F'n'A!

My Crazy Life in Rock and Blues

Published by:
Blooming Twig Books
New York / Tulsa
www.bloomingtwig.com

Hardcover: ISBN: 978-1-61343-100-9
Paperback: ISBN: 978-1-61343-099-6
eBook: ISBN: 978-1-61343-098-9

First Edition
Printed in the United States of America.

Cover design by Kristina Tosic
Front cover photo by Anne Sutherland
Back cover art by Danden Jensen

Acknowledgements
F 'n' A! My Crazy Life in Rock and Blues

First of all, I want to thank my publisher, Kent Gustavson, PhD, of Blooming Twig Books, for his foresight in understanding the importance of a book written about musicians who spend their lives in the background, while supporting stars of rock, blues, R&B and other styles of music, both on stage and in recording studios, yet receiving little or no recognition. Special thanks to my editor, Daphne Tuccitto, for her excellent work with my manuscript, Shannon Brown, for her help with my book's layout, graphic artist Kristina Tosic, for her meaningful cover design, and Swedish artist Danden Jensen, for his painting on the book's back cover. Also, special thanks to my friend and internationally-acclaimed author and musician, Professor Dean Alger, who recommended my book to Blooming Twig.

I want to thank bandleader Larry Lynne, who gave me my first steady job in professional music when I was eighteen years old, and taught me how to play with a band. Without Larry's help, I'd have just been a kid, playing piano for my friends in their parents' living rooms.

Special thanks goes to Joey D. Vieira, (co-star in Mel Gibson's epic film, *The Patriot*), my close friend and former manager, who has believed in my music since he heard me playing on the Sunset Strip in 1966 and encouraged me to write this book. Also, my dear friend, sax player Tom Fabré, who taught me to graduate from a little spinet organ to the mighty Hammond B3, and my loving grandparents, Don and Cora Huntzinger, who made payments on my organ when I was broke, yet always believed in my music. Extra thanks to my wonderful piano teacher, Marian Howard, who taught me the basics of piano when I was nine years old, and her daughter, Marilyn, who showed me a left-hand boogie riff that led to my love for the blues.

I want to thank Delaney and Bonnie Bramlett, Etta James, Howlin' Wolf, Sonny Boy Williamson, Allen Toussaint, Dr. John, Freddy Fender, Ernie K-Doe, Jimmy McGriff, "Groove" Holmes, the Dukes of Dixieland and all the "name" artists I've been honored to work with during my life. I also want to thank drummers Eddie Tururi and Paul Edwards, organists Herbert Noord and Albert & Carol Ratcliffe, Richard Nowak and guitarist/attorney Vince Megna for prompting me to write my memoirs.

Thanks to my son and daughter, Craig and Kelli Sutherland, for their love and encouragement. Most importantly, I want to thank my wife, Anne, for walking with me, hand-in-hand, from the flames of drug-induced hell to the rolling, heather-covered fields of Scotland. Never once, even when we lived in poverty, did she suggest (or allow) me to give up music and get a "regular" job! When I offered to go to law school at USC, she said, "I didn't marry a lawyer; I married a musician!"

For Anne

You are a rainbow, you are the wind

You are the singing of a mockingbird

You are the flowers, you are my friend

You are the stars in the desert sky

Contents

F'n'A!

My Crazy Life in Rock and Blues

By
Rick Allen

2015
Blooming Twig Books
New York / Tulsa

Chapter 1

Breakfast with Howlin' Wolf

The sky was steely gray when we arrived at the Detroit airport on a cold January morning. Dirty soot-stained snow lined the streets on our taxi ride to the Shelby Hotel where we were scheduled to perform. It was 1975, and I was on tour as keyboard player with Don Preston, lead guitarist from the recent breakup of Leon Russell and the Shelter People. Don was promoting his first solo album *Been Here All the Time*, and Detroit was fifth on the rock club circuit. We had already played Tulsa, Lansing, Allentown, and St. Louis, before we headed for New York City, Washington, D.C., and other cities on the East Coast. But Detroit in wintertime topped the list for the ugliest.

As our taxi passed a gigantic replica of a truck tire that rose close to a hundred feet in the air, our drummer Chuck Blackwell turned to the cabbie and said, "Someone should take dynamite and blow that piece of shit to pieces!" I burst out laughing, but the cabbie remained silent. I think he was proud of that big tire.

We had played other northern industrial cities in the wintertime, all of them dingy and depressing, but Detroit felt like an umbrella of gloom had enveloped the entire town. Amid this veil of desolation, a ray of sunshine was about to enter my life. When we reached the hotel, I couldn't believe my eyes. On the marquis was *Howlin' Wolf!* I'd loved his music since I was a kid and couldn't believe we were playing the same venue. It would be my first chance to see him perform in person. I had played many cities throughout the U.S., but an almost surreal experience was waiting for me in Detroit.

After I checked into my room and unpacked my suitcase, I went to the hotel's restaurant for a late breakfast. The café was almost empty, but I saw an elderly black man who looked like Howlin' Wolf sitting alone. After some hesitation, I walked over to his table. The big man looked at me and smiled and I asked, "Sir, are you Howlin' Wolf?" He nodded and said, "Yeah, they call me Wolf." When I mentioned I was a musician, he growled, "Hey man, have a seat!" It's difficult to remember what he ordered, but I think it was a stack of pancakes. As for me, I ordered my usual hash browns, sausage, and toast. My encounter with Wolf seems like a dream. *Breakfast at Tiffany's* was a nice fantasy, but breakfast with Howlin' Wolf was an unbelievable reality.

I didn't know how to address this living legend. "Mr. Wolf" or his birth name Chester Burnett were out of the question, so I just called him "Sir." I told him his music was a major influence on my playing, and when I said I loved the blues he said, "Man, the blues been good to me! The blues helped me make a good living." He also said that his piano player had left the band and flown off to Alaska. (If the piano player had quit Wolf in the middle of a gig, Alaska would have been a good place to hide. Wolf was a big man, six foot six, weighed close to three hundred pounds and was known to have a bad temper.) Wolf's next words hit me like *Smokestack Lightnin'*. He said, "Man, I got three shows tonight. Would you like to play piano?" Playing with Howlin' Wolf was the chance of a lifetime. He didn't say anything about money, and to ask Wolf to pay me would have been unthinkable. Not even Stevie Ray or Clapton would have dared. Just playing with Howlin' Wolf would be the highest honor for any musician.

A large nightclub called The Savoy was located in the basement of our hotel. When it was close to showtime, I entered the club with our tenor sax player, Bud Deal, but Wolf was nowhere to be seen. We took a seat at the bar and waited, sipping beers. On the other side of the room was an elevated bandstand. A grand piano was on the floor at stage right. I downed a few more beers to gain a modicum of courage, as I needed all the courage I could muster to play with Wolf and his band of Chicago blues musicians. I don't remember the names of the drummer and bass player, but the lead guitarist was Hubert Sumlin, who had played on countless hit records with Muddy Waters, Little Walter, Etta James, Sonny Boy Williamson, Howlin' Wolf, and many others. It was an ominous challenge to play with these formidable blues masters.

When I saw Wolf and his band walking toward the bandstand, I took my seat at the piano. Since the piano was on the floor, it would be impossible for the band members to tell me the keys of Wolf's songs from the stage. Wolf sat on a fold-up chair in front of the bandstand, about ten feet from me. With guitar in hand, he began to sing his famous song "Evil," a song about a husband who's worried that another *mule* (a man) is *kickin' in his stall* (sleeping with his wife). I put my ear close to the piano, searched for the correct key, then joined in with the band.

After I had overcome most of my fear, it was fun playing Wolf's songs like "Spoonful," "Back Door Man," and "Forty-Four." Saving the best for last, Wolf closed each set with his personal and heartrending version of "Goin' Down Slow," obviously dedicated to his mother who had hurt him deeply. She was never proud of his accomplishments, called his music "sinful," and refused to accept money from her famous son. As he sang the closing lyrics *"Please write my mama/ Tell her the shape I'm in/ Ask her to pray for me/ Forgive me for my sins,"* I could see this tower of a man wiping tears from his eyes.

From where Wolf was sitting, he was able to watch me. He seemed to be staring, perhaps even glaring at me, but I couldn't tell what he was thinking. There was never a smile, only an analytical stare as a waitress supplied me with a constant flow of free beer. Many years later I learned that Wolf had an ironclad rule against musicians drinking on stage. He didn't care if they drank during their breaks but never allowed them to drink while performing. For years I thought that Wolf was staring because he didn't like my playing. I wish he'd told me about his drinking rule, but due to this misunderstanding, I was afraid to speak to him during our breaks, and kept my distance while he signed autographs on the other side of the room. I remember thinking, "If Wolf insults my playing, I'll never believe in myself again."

Later I learned that if Wolf didn't like a musician's playing, he'd kick him off the stage. He'd grab the microphone and say, "Get the hell outta here!" even to famous blues musicians like Little Walter. If Wolf had hated my playing, he'd have never allowed me to play more than a few songs, but he let me play all night. To have *survived* three shows in the jaws of The Wolf was my reward.

Wolf died almost a year later, and my wife and I played his music most of that day. But he'd left me with a priceless legacy. Just as world leaders are honored to dine with kings and queens, I'd played a gig and had breakfast with the great Howlin' Wolf!

Chapter 2

Who is Ritchie Valens?

"EL MONTE LEGION STADIUM, SATURDAY NIGHT! BE THERE OR BE SQUARE!"

Hollywood deejay Art Laboe was on the radio. It's a familiar rock 'n' roll story. A boy listening to loud music stands at the bathroom mirror, combing his hair, getting ready to go out with his friends. Suddenly the bathroom door bursts open. "Turn off that screaming garbage NOW!" says his father—my six-foot-four Irish father.

My dad and I never saw eye-to-eye about *anything* when I was a teenager. Our relationship can best be described as a mix of ambivalence, fear on my part, and mutual animosity. Almost *too* intelligent, my father was a sad dreamer. He'd been an extra in many movies, including *City Lights* with Charlie Chaplin, but considered himself a failure for not getting bigger roles. Next he tried screenwriting, only to receive letters of rejection. Later on he invented a machine for the military, capable of drilling holes through solid concrete. He sold our family home to finance a prototype, took it to Washington, D.C. with great expectations, but it was rejected by the Pentagon. In spite of these failures, he was an excellent salesman, working periodically as sales manager for Los Angeles manufacturers of industrial machinery. I say "periodically" because recurrent bouts of rheumatism rendered him bedridden for weeks, missing work and losing jobs. Always the gentleman, he never left home without wearing a dark blue suit and appropriate necktie, sometimes going to work on crutches.

When I emerged from the bathroom in my Pachuco clothes and hairstyle, the "coolest" things happening in Southern California at the time, my father said, "Why do you comb your hair like that? You look like a fairy." At fifteen, I hated my curly hair and the rest of my tall, skinny body. I had spent almost an hour using Butch Wax to comb my hair into a waterfall with a duck-tail in the back. Just when I thought I was *almost* "lookin' good," my father cut me down. As I was walking out the front door, he said, "You're not *half* as important as you think you are!" His words still resonate with me, but I was determined to prove him wrong.

My friends and I were going to an R&B show in El Monte, just north of my hometown of Whittier. Once home to Olympic sports events, El Monte Legion Stadium was *the place* for live rhythm and blues. Most of us weren't old enough to drive, so an older classmate took us in his red '52 Ford. Lower in the front, the car bounced as it rolled the streets. "Nosed and decked," the manufacturer's insignias had been removed from the hood and trunk, the holes filled with Bondo and sprayed with gray primer. The dashboard was covered with spiderweb pinstriping, and the seats were red tuck & roll, installed by a cheap upholstery shop in Tijuana.

I had been to El Monte Legion Stadium before to see the great R&B performers of the day: Johnny "Guitar" Watson, Don and Dewey, Johnny Otis, Sonny Knight, The Penguins, The Coasters, and many more. I dreamed of playing with them one day, never quite believing my good fortune when I was on stage with most of them a few years later.

My friends and I were "gringo vatos," white kids in Pachuco clothes. We wore khaki pants, Sir Guy shirts buttoned to the top, and black Stacy Adams shoes, spit-shined until we could see our reflections in the toes. We fit in with the Mexican-American crowd and the Chicano kids never bothered us. Sometimes we saw switchblade fights in the parking lot but kept our distance. We were there to hear the music, meet girls, and dance.

In my case, it was the music that drew me to El Monte. While other kids danced I stood in front of the stage watching the singers and musicians. They were the coolest people I had ever seen. Black singers with hair piled high, guitar and bass players with their instruments hanging to their knees. Some of them were tall and skinny like me, but if they played music, they were stars! More than anything in the world, I wanted to be on that stage.

Teenage kids in Los Angeles didn't like most "white music." We listened to Elvis and Buddy Holly but couldn't stand Pat Boone and others like him. When the Big Bopper came on stage that night in El Monte with a toy telephone and sang "Chantilly Lace," a friend of mine burst out laughing in disgust. After the Big Bopper finished his set, a chubby Mexican teenager climbed up to the stage. I wondered what was happening. Where were the black performers? What was this shy-looking boy doing at El Monte Legion Stadium? Nobody paid much attention to him. I watched as he plugged his guitar into a small amplifier and walked up to the microphone. I expected the worst. All of a sudden, he started singing a song that struck me like a jolt of electricity: *"Well, come on let's go, let's go, let's go little darlin'."*

Ritchie Valens wasn't famous—yet. He walked to the stage alone and left the stage alone. No bodyguards, no autograph seekers. I was standing in his path to the dressing room when I stopped him and said, "Man, I love your music." We shook hands, and I'll never forget his eyes. They looked straight into my soul. Both magical and sad, they seemed to say, "I know you! You're a musician." Even more profound was a possible awareness of his own destiny, that his eyes revealed his unavoidable fate. Maybe this impression is completely wrong, and he was just missing his girlfriend Donna, later immortalized in song. I'll never know the answer, but I've met many famous people, yet never had this same feeling.

Chapter 3

First Gig, Age 15
Don Preston

When I returned to Whittier High the following Monday, I told some friends that I'd heard a great new singer named Ritchie Valens at El Monte Legion Stadium. One of my friends said, "Don't you know that Don Preston plays guitar at El Monte? He's probably played with that guy." Don Preston and I attended the same school and even shared a Spanish class, but I didn't know him personally. I had no idea he was a musician nor that he played guitar with R&B stars.

Excited, I stopped Don in the hallway after Spanish class and began talking about music. When I told him I played rhythm and blues piano, Don said he would like to hear my music. After school, as we walked to his house, Don told me he had been playing with Little Julian Herrera, singer on "Those Lonely Nights," and with Don Julian and the Meadowlarks, who recorded the Doo-Wop song, "Heaven and Paradise." Those artists were very famous in Southern California.

There was a spinet piano in Don's parents' living room. I didn't like spinets because they were too small to project the loud volume I wanted, but I played it as best I could. Don smiled and said, "You play like Jerry Lee Lewis!" I didn't know whether to take that as a compliment or an insult. Jerry Lee was a great piano player, but he was white! I didn't want to sound like a white boy; I wanted to sound black like Fats Domino. On reflection, I think Don meant to compliment me.

From the living room we migrated to Don's bedroom where he kept his Gretsch electric guitar and a small amplifier. He picked up the guitar and played some interesting chords and blues licks, and even showed me his "secret" way of playing the classic instrumental "Honky Tonk" by Bill Doggett. Little did I realize that one day I'd play organ with Clifford Scott, the tenor sax player on "Honky Tonk." Scott's solos on that record have been copied, note for note, by almost every sax player on earth.

When Preston was attending Whittier High, he didn't look like a musician. He wore clothes that weren't cool, with black high-top tennis shoes and Levi's buckled above his waist. He looked more like a hillbilly kid than a performer. But at age sixteen, Preston was one of the best young R&B guitar players in Southern California. He often played with local stars as well as nationally known artists like The Coasters, Chuck Berry, Jerry Lee Lewis, and my new hero, Ritchie Valens!

In the late 1950s, Preston played in a band called The Phantoms. Radio commercials claimed the musicians were so famous that they needed to hide their identities. They came on stage dressed in masks and costumes like the Phantom comic book character. Their audiences never realized that the band consisted of teenage musicians from Whittier and East L.A.

Preston had (and continues to have) a unique style of guitar playing. Left-handed, but unlike many lefties who play guitar upside down with the neck to their right, he plays guitar in the right-handed position, the neck to his left. This puts his most coordinated fingers on the frets rather than on the guitar pick. As a result, he's better able to bend and stretch strings, which makes his guitar sing like a violin. Beautiful soaring notes that bend, curl, and moan like the voices of gospel singers.

Soon after my visit to his home, Don called and asked if I'd like to play a gig with his band. I couldn't believe my ears! Don wanted me to meet him, along with his sax player and drummer for a rehearsal at the old Bailey Building in Whittier, an ancient two-story structure that had once served as a grammar school. We found a room with a piano in the corner, and went over some songs together. I'd never played with other musicians before, and some of the keys were difficult for me. I wasn't used to playing in the guitar keys of *E* and *A*, and it was especially hard for me to play in *B flat*. But I played well enough to convince Don that I could handle the job. Some tunes were four-chord Doo-Wop songs like "Earth Angel" by The Penguins, while the others were three-chord blues like "Sweet Little Angel" by B. B. King. The other musicians were about my age but had experience playing gigs around L.A. I was the new kid on the block. Up until this point, I'd just been jamming on piano for my friends.

The gig was for a Saturday night dance at Laguna Park Civic Center in East L.A. Don said we would be opening for Don Julian and the Meadowlarks, but Don Julian never showed up. I think Preston was just trying to impress me with a "big name" artist who never intended to play in the first place.

I told my parents I'd been hired to play my first professional gig, but they weren't interested. They never considered going to the dance to hear me play. My parents hated my music, and gave me all the discouragement, criticism, and negativity they could muster. I still remember my father saying, "You'll never make it, playing that nigger music," to which I responded, "When I get older, my generation will grow older with me. They'll want to hear the style of music they grew up with, not the old standards from your generation. They'll want to hear Little Richard and Fats Domino, not Frank Sinatra and Benny Goodman." Obviously, time has proven me to be correct.

Don Preston drove me to Laguna Park for the first gig of my life. A medium-sized recreational building on the park grounds with capacity for several hundred people, it was often used for live shows featuring local musicians and singers. We entered the dressing room that was actually a kitchen, with stoves, steel sinks, and a dishwashing machine, and changed into some fancy shirts that Don had brought for the band and himself. The shirts were light blue and covered with sequins that sparkled in the light, with big billowy sleeves that almost reached our hands. We wore our own dark slacks and black shoes. I was thrilled to wear that "flashy" shirt and felt like a real musician for the first time in my life, but I was also scared to death! Outside the "dressing room" were over one hundred teenage kids, waiting to hear us play.

The stage was small. In one corner was an upright piano waiting for my terrified fingers. There was a microphone inside the piano, connected to the P.A. system. Our drummer sat behind me while Don and the sax player stood in front. It was time to start the music. Fear and excitement made my hands tremble as we began the show with Bill Doggett's "Honky Tonk," one of the songs we'd rehearsed in Whittier. I'd memorized the intro, the familiar three-chord blues changes, the "breaks" and the coda (song ending). The tenor sax honked the familiar melody, and Don's solos soared above the crowd. The audience applauded and cheered.

My fears abated, I found myself in "Musician's Heaven." I had never felt so happy in my young life. It was a much *higher* high than T-Bird wine, and even more exciting than making out with pretty girls. It was everything I'd ever wanted. I don't remember how much money I was paid after the gig, but it was probably five or ten dollars. It is said that an artist becomes professional when he's paid for his work, so I guess I became a professional that night in East L.A. at age fifteen.

After the show, teenage girls stampeded our dressing room. They carried pens and little pieces of paper and wanted autographs. Instead of flocking to Don, most of the girls gathered around me! As far as they were concerned, I was the star of the show. I was both flattered and embarrassed. It would be fifteen years before Don Preston hired me again, and I've always wondered if it was because I didn't play well enough that night or because of the girls who treated me more like Elvis than just a nervous piano player.

Musically speaking, I was born in the right place at the right time. In late 1950s and early 1960s Los Angeles, my friends and I listened to black radio stations, saw the stars of R&B, Doo-Wop and the blues in live shows, and drove to South Central L.A. to buy their music. Records by Muddy Waters, Sonny Boy Williamson, John Lee Hooker, Buddy Guy, Otis Rush, Jimmy Reed, and Howlin' Wolf became my teachers. And man, did my parents hate those records!

My mother had a collection of classical 78s of Chopin, Bach, Beethoven, and other composers. She knew I had musical talent and set her sights on my becoming a classical pianist. A lover of the fine arts, my mother made sure I was exposed to classical music at a young age. She took me to hear symphony orchestras in Los Angeles and made me listen to her records, but fate would take me down a very different path.

My first experience with live music was at my grandparents' home in Upland, California. In their living room, next to a large 1940's vintage radio, stood a Victorian upright piano. Although beautiful to me, it was actually quite ugly, with massive scrolling and a round piano stool with Gargoyle feet. Whenever my grandmother played that piano, I was spellbound. I never banged on the keys when she played like most kids do. I watched in awe as her hands danced across the keys, lightly touching the black and white pieces of ivory and wood. She played beautiful Scottish ballads like "Annie Laurie" and "Loch Lomond." Watching my grandmother play was my first inspiration to play the piano, but an experience with an organist would present an even more fascinating challenge.

As a child, my grandfather often took me for walks around the little town of Upland. When I was about five years old, we passed by an ivy-covered Episcopal Church and heard the sounds of music. Through a side door, we stepped inside and climbed a flight of stairs to the loft, where a pretty lady was playing an organ. She turned, smiled at me, and went on playing until the piece was finished. She could see that I was enchanted by the organ and asked if I'd like to touch the keyboard. She said I could play just one note, and pointed to a certain key. In a moment of both terror and excitement, I lightly touched the key and could hear the incredible power of the instrument boom and echo through the cavernous church. It was a turning point in my musical life. The organ had so many more keys and sounds than my grandmother's piano! Two or three keyboards for the hands and strange-looking wooden pedals for the feet. In my young mind, I dreamed of someday playing such an amazing instrument.

When I was nine years old, my grandmother's big upright piano was moved from storage to my bedroom in Whittier. I was excited to have the piano and wanted to learn to play. My mother, who believed in my musical talent, arranged for me to take lessons from her best friend, Marian Howard, who taught me scales, correct fingering, chord structures and gave me a beginner's John W. Schaum piano book. When my teacher demonstrated how a song should be played, I memorized it and played it by ear while pretending to read the notes. I used this trick with all the songs in my book and received gold stars on every page. It was much easier to play by ear, and I didn't realize that most people were unable to do this. I didn't stop with the songs in my piano book, and taught myself to play songs I heard on the radio and the hymns we sang in church.

One day after a piano lesson, my teacher's teenage daughter Marilyn showed me a left-hand boogie pattern. Like a genie released from a bottle, piano boogies brought out my hidden ability to improvise solos, an absolute necessity for playing jazz, rock, and the blues. Almost immediately, I was able to play the theme of a song while playing a left-hand boogie riff, and then "take off" with improvised right-hand solos. I even turned religious hymns like "The Old Rugged Cross" into boogies, which upset my mother but made the kids snicker. Eventually, I learned "When the Saints Go Marching In." "Play the Saints, Ricky," was a constant request from my friends.

About this time, I began listening to rhythm and blues on the radio and was hooked for life. Soon I was playing Fats Domino's "Blueberry Hill" and "Blue Monday" on piano. Next I discovered Little Richard, another piano player and the most exciting singer I had ever heard. I couldn't sing like Richard, but I could play his piano riffs. I cut lawns and delivered newspapers to buy his records and learned to play them on piano while my parents were at work.

I wasn't allowed to play rhythm and blues when my parents were home, so I often practiced at friends' homes, empty churches, and the YMCA. I was a tall, skinny boy with many complexes, but playing music made me popular with other kids. Music was the only thing that made me feel special. Once I was arrested in Huntington Beach for playing blues on a pipe organ in a Catholic Church. The police handcuffed me and took me to Orange County Juvenile Hall in Santa Ana, where I was locked in a cell. My father picked me up the next day and refused to speak to me as we rode home to Whittier. Maybe I wouldn't have been arrested had I been playing "Ave Maria" instead of "Bright Lights, Big City" by Jimmy Reed.

Chapter 4

Almost a member of The Beach Boys

Car Clubs, Gang Wars

Car clubs were popular with teenagers in Southern California, and Whittier was no exception. I was excited when my friends, Steve Korthoff and Gene Aquino sponsored my membership in a club called "The Road Gamblers." Behind closed doors, my name was put up for a vote, and I was afraid I might be rejected. After about half an hour, Steve walked up to me and said, "Welcome to The Road Gamblers, Rick. And by the way, you were elected vice president." I was thrilled beyond words. As a member, I got to wear a black jacket with an insignia on the back: a 1932 Ford, two dice, and the inscription, "Road Gamblers, Southern California." I also got a gold plaque for the rear window of my 1948 Chevy. I loved wearing that jacket, because it showed that I was part of something bigger than myself, and that bullies who messed with me were messing with an entire club of strong and protective guys.

At almost every Road Gamblers' meeting in an old schoolhouse called the Bailey Building, Steve Korthoff talked about his cousins who were putting a band together and needed a piano player. He wanted me to meet them at their home in Hawthorne, but I wasn't interested. His cousins were rehearsing in their parents' garage and I got the impression they were just a bunch of kids. I wanted to keep playing rhythm and blues with Don Preston, who was already playing important gigs around L.A. It turned out that Steve's cousins were Brian, Dennis, and Carl Wilson. A few years later, they called themselves The Beach Boys. That was my first chance to become rich and famous. When I think about this missed opportunity, I remind myself that I've never liked The Beach Boys' music. No feeling and no soul, it was fishbelly white. Legend has it that Mississippi bluesman Robert Johnson sold his soul to the devil at "The Crossroads" to become a great guitar player. It would have been hell on earth for me to sell my soul to The Beach Boys for money and fame.

The Road Gamblers weren't the only car club in Whittier. There was a girls' club called "Satan's Daughters" and another boys' club called "The Block Busters." Friction developed between members of the two boys' clubs, and the decision was made to have a gang war. The fight was to take place on a Saturday night at Penn Park in Whittier, a dark and secluded area.

I was afraid of the gang war because I was too weak and skinny to fight. No matter my fear, I was a member of The Road Gamblers and had to stand with them. I decided to fight as best I could, although I expected to get a beating. In those days, some kids in Whittier carried switchblade knives, can openers (called church keys), and solid metal objects called "fist fillers." On the night of the fight, I brought a rake handle that I found in someone's trash. There was a boy in The Block Busters who especially hated my guts. I knew he would be waiting.

Upon reaching Penn Park, we were immediately surrounded by police cars with flashing red lights. The wailing sound of sirens filled the night air. Obviously, someone had informed the cops about the fight. I quickly discarded my rake handle, throwing it into some nearby bushes. Members of both car clubs were ordered to drive to the old Bailey Building on Hadley Street and meet at the boxing ring in the basement. Our sponsor, Sergeant Bill Spencer of the Whittier Police Department, was wise enough to turn a dangerous gang war into a sports event.

The gymnasium at the Bailey Building was a dusty remnant of the past.

There were rusty barbells, weighted ropes for building muscles, and strange wooden rungs on the walls. In the center of the gym was a boxing ring. Its drooping brown ropes were cracked and withered with age. A light bulb hung over the ring, casting a yellow hue upon the faded ugly canvas. There was no piano to help me. Nothing but false courage and a feeling of hopeless fate. I took a seat with my Road Gambler friends on one side of the ring, while on the opposite side sat our rival club, The Block Busters. Sergeant Spencer selected members from each club to face off in one-round bouts. Boys with particular grudges were allowed to fight first. Each round lasted until a boy was down for the count of ten seconds.

As expected, the kid from The Block Busters who hated my very existence picked me as his opponent. I climbed through the ropes and into the ring. A police referee laced enormous brown boxing gloves on my hands, a bell rang, and the fight was on. For once, being tall and skinny became an advantage. My arms were much longer than those of my enemy, and my gloves were able to make frequent contact with his face. This irritated him, and he decided to charge me like a bull. This threw him off balance, and he fell to the mat. He got to his feet and tried to charge again. I kept swinging at his head. He slipped and fell to the mat a second time. His falls were making me look pretty good. When my opponent got to his feet a second time, I attacked him like a raging windmill.

Suddenly, there was a sickening, wet thump in my right shoulder, and my arm became paralyzed. I instinctively grabbed my injured arm with my left-hand glove and yelled for help. My opponent used this opportunity to hit me as many times as he could until the referee stopped the fight. I was driven to the Murphy Memorial Hospital in a police car and entered the emergency room.

The doctors could easily see that my right shoulder was dislocated. I was in great pain, but the doctors couldn't help me without my parents' consent. My father and mother were called on the telephone. It was late at night, and they were sleeping. I lay on a stretcher in agony for over an hour, waiting for my parents. I was given no medication to ease the suffering. After my parents arrived, I was given a shot of morphine and placed upon an operating table. A doctor began to manipulate my helpless arm. Even with morphine, it was a painful procedure. I was relieved to hear a meaty "thump" as my shoulder popped back into its socket.

After a few days at home, I returned to school to learn that my boxing opponent had been bragging that he'd won the fight by "knocking my shoulder out of joint." Although he was lying, I would never prove him wrong. My boxing days were over. From that day forth, my boxing ring would be the stage and my opponents would be other keyboard players.

Chapter 5

On the Road, Age 18

At age seventeen, with failing grades in high school and a painful break-up with my girlfriend, I convinced my parents to allow me to quit school and join the Navy. The military helped to tame my wild ways, and I was honorably discharged after one year's service due to another shoulder injury, caused by rough-housing with a friend named Lyle Lashbrook.

After several months of confusion over what to do with my life, I received a telephone call from Larry Lynne, leader of one of Milwaukee's most popular bands, The Bonnevilles. Larry and I had become friends when I was stationed at Great Lakes Naval Training Center in Illinois and spent my liberty weekends in Milwaukee, often "sitting in" on piano with The Bonnevilles. He explained that he was making some changes in the group and wanted me to replace his keyboard player. I was excited and thrilled beyond belief. This was my chance to be a real professional.

My grandmother gave me $100 for plane fare and Grandpa gave me a little money for food. I flew from Los Angeles to Chicago and took a train to Milwaukee, ragged suitcase in hand. Unfortunately, there was nothing in my suitcase to prepare me for the Wisconsin winter. Larry met me at the Milwaukee train station, and as I walked to his car I could hear ice cracking beneath my feet. My light jacket offered no protection from the bitter cold. Eventually, Larry gave me an old black overcoat. I was over six feet tall and Larry was much shorter, so the coat barely reached my knees. Nevertheless, I was glad to wear it.

Young men in Milwaukee dressed much better than those in California. While L.A. boys wore blue jeans or khakis, their Milwaukee counterparts were wearing high-style suits from New York. Fancy shirts with French cuffs, sparkling cufflinks, and Italian shoes. My clothes made me feel like a garbage man invited to a banquet. I looked so pathetic that a friend of The Bonnevilles gave me one of his old brown suits. The jacket was too large and the shoulders slumped, but it was in the "high fashion" style of Milwaukee men's clothing.

My first unpleasant surprise came when Larry told me I'd be staying at the home of Judy Lemke, teenage president of The Bonnevilles' fan club. I remembered her from hanging out with The Bonnevilles during my Navy days. A nice girl, Judy was still attending high school and living with her parents in a working-class neighborhood. This wasn't what I'd expected when I left California, as I took it for granted I'd be staying with Larry. A stranger from a distant land, I was assigned a cot in the Lemkes' basement next to a water heater, but after two days I was asked to leave. Judy's father was a "meat and potatoes" factory worker with no patience for an almost penniless musician to share his hard-earned food. He told me I'd have to pay room and board or move out of his house.

I called Larry and told him I needed a place to stay. After all, he'd brought me over 2,000 miles from home. Reluctantly, he agreed to let me stay with him at a house owned by his parents; reluctant because the kitchen pantry was bare, the refrigerator empty, and Larry was broke. His mother and father kept the house as an investment while living in an apartment above their Milwaukee tavern. I hadn't expected to starve as a new member of the locally-famous Bonnevilles.

A much more devastating surprise was to learn that The Bonnevilles no longer existed! The band had broken up. While I was blindsided by Larry's somewhat misleading offer when I was in California, I had no choice but to stay in Milwaukee. Larry was an incredible singer, front man, and guitarist, and I had faith that we'd have a brighter future. I was willing to endure *anything* to become a real musician.

Occasionally my grandparents sent me a little money, but I often went to bed without dinner. I remember waking up so hungry that I ventured into Larry's kitchen in search of a scrap of bread. All I found was a can of Hills Bros. coffee. I got a spoon, ate some coffee, but it stuck in my throat and made me vomit into the kitchen sink. The next day, after searching every dresser drawer in the house, Larry found enough loose change to buy a few glazed donuts at a Big Boy restaurant. Man, I was so hungry that those donuts tasted as good as T-bone steaks. About a week later, Larry landed a Saturday night gig at a club called The Galaxy in Cudahy, Wisconsin. He hired the bass player and drummer from the disbanded Bonnevilles, and I was hired to play piano. It would be my first club gig. I played well on my newly-acquired Wurlitzer electric piano, got a good reaction from the audience, and earned fifteen dollars! I could eat chili and crackers at Big Boy's and fifteen-cent hamburgers at George Webb's, a local burger chain.

I'd never been satisfied playing an acoustic piano. When I lived with my parents in Whittier, I stuck thumbtacks into the hammers and put a microphone inside the piano, which I connected to my parents' powerful hi-fi record player. This amplified the piano, and I was able to play solos based on runs and individual notes rather than chords. I'd already learned the chord-based styles of Huey "Piano" Smith and Fats Domino, but I wanted something more. I wanted to play sustained notes like blues guitar players. My determination to play guitar-type single-note solos on the keyboard was the beginning of my Hammond B3 style.

From records like *What'd I Say*, I discovered that Ray Charles was playing a Wurlitzer electric piano. It was exactly what I wanted! It had a mean, funky tone and played through an amplifier, loud enough for an audience to hear every note! In Milwaukee, Larry's brother co-signed with me to buy a Wurlitzer, and Larry lent me a Fender amplifier. Soon we began rehearsing in Larry's living room.

Larry hired Paul Edwards to be our drummer. A good musician, we became friends and shared many wild adventures. Larry also hired an acne-faced bass player named John, although he was soon replaced by

Tom Hahn, a much better musician. In November of 1961, we signed with Artists Corporation of America, a Milwaukee-based agency that booked bands throughout the Midwest. With an advance from the agency, we rented tuxedos, dress shirts, and patent leather shoes. Professional 8x10 photos were taken, I joined the musician's union and we were ready to hit the road.

Our first gig was at the Top Hat Lounge in Kankakee, Illinois, where we were booked for two weeks. It was late November, and we ate our Thanksgiving turkey dinners at a Walgreens drugstore across the street from the Top Hat. We sat at a malt-shop counter on red and silver stools, and after many years I still have fond memories of that meal. The gravy was a ghastly yellow, but it was great to be able to eat in restaurants, no matter how pathetic, with money I had earned playing music.

In every Midwestern town we played, our band was advertised in local newspapers. In most cases, these ads included pictures of our group. I started a scrapbook, just as my father had done when he was an actor. I mailed news clippings and 8x10 glossy photos to my parents, thinking they might be proud of me. Apparently they felt otherwise, and never framed or hung the pictures anywhere in their home. Instead my parents criticized the photographs, saying my hair was too long and my expression unbecoming. The newspaper clippings and reviews went to the bottom of a dresser drawer or to the trash. I was never to receive a compliment from my parents.

It was fun being on the road with the new Bonnevilles. I was only eighteen, but managed to get an Illinois driver's license that put my age at twenty-one, the required age to play nightclubs. We had a great time with booze, music, and women. In fact, we had so much fun that we were often fired from our gigs. This usually happened in small hick towns, where jealous boyfriends took pleasure in harassing our band, sometimes leading to police intervention. Those young men couldn't compete with city boys from Milwaukee, dressed in tuxedos and playing good music. At the Top Hat Lounge, a man hit me in the mouth while I was playing piano. In Muncie, Indiana, a group of rednecks sat in front of the stage, throwing popcorn at the band and flashing pocket knives. We needed a police escort to leave the club.

After Muncie, our next engagement was at the Venice Nite Club in Ishpeming, Michigan. Of all the strange names of towns in the Midwest, this was the funniest I'd ever heard. It was a long drive from Indiana to Upper Michigan, and by the time we got to Ishpeming, it was late at night. The town was fast asleep and Ishpeming's only hotel was closed until morning. It was a dark and freezing December night, but I had a bright idea.

All four members of The Bonnevilles walked into the Ishpeming Police Station and asked if we could spend the night in jail. The desk sergeant's eyelids flipped open in disbelief. Four disheveled musicians with messed-up Pompadour haircuts were asking to sleep in jail? "Let me get this straight," the sergeant said in his Michigan accent, "Youz guys really want to sleep in jail cells? Well, I guess that can be arranged, but we'll have to lock youz up 'til morning. That's the rules, eh?" We agreed and were assigned two jail cells. Paul and I were locked in one cell, Larry and our bass player in another. The bars slammed shut, and The Bonnevilles slept. In the morning, our cells were unlocked and we were served pancakes on tin plates. A real "Jailhouse Rock" breakfast. We thanked the cops for their hospitality and invited them to hear us play at the Venice Club. I don't know if any of them came because they would have been wearing civilian clothes, and we wouldn't have recognized them.

Along with the rising sun, the doors to the "city" were re-opened for business and we checked into Ishpeming's only hotel, a brownstone monstrosity probably built before the Civil War. It was at this hotel that drummer Paul tossed a smoke bomb into the coal furnace and filled the building with yellow fog. The hotel manager suspected us, since we were the only youngsters in his hotel, and he called the police. When the cops arrived and knocked on our door, we told them we had no idea where the smoke came from. Maybe there was something wrong with the furnace? I remember telling them, "We're not just musicians, we're college students, taking a year off to make a little money. We'd never do anything like smoke out a hotel. We're good citizens." The cops seemed to believe this line. They might still be searching for the *real* smoke-bomber!

I rode from gig to gig with Paul in his 1955 red Mercury, drums in the back seat, my electric piano in the trunk. Paul had the habit of falling asleep at the wheel. In northern Wisconsin, he crashed off the road into a snow bank. Drums flew from the back seat to the front, hitting us both in the head. Paul woke up, puzzled. We hired a farmer to pull the car from the snow with his pickup truck.

In southern Illinois, Paul drifted off to sleep and crashed off the highway onto some railroad tracks. All four tires were flattened from the impact. The drums flew from the back seat and once again, Paul woke up with a startled look on his face as if to say, "What the hell happened?"

In central Indiana, Paul nodded off and the car began drifting across the double lines to the wrong side of the highway. I reached over and righted the steering wheel, while yelling at Paul to wake up. Almost immediately, the police were upon us, lights flashing and siren blaring. Paul was arrested and ordered to appear before a small-town judge. "Court" was held in a greasy spoon café. The judge sat at a formica-topped table, eating potato chips and drinking coffee. He fined Paul twenty dollars and threatened to throw me in jail for contempt because I said the fine was too high. Twenty dollars was a lot of money in 1961. I often asked Paul to let me drive, or at least take turns, but to no avail.

After almost a year on the road in the Midwest, I thought we were musically ready for California. I was sick of the cold weather and snow, and longed for the California sunshine. Los Angeles was my home turf, and I was anxious to show off to my friends. I had no problem convincing the other band members that we should head for the West Coast. I called the L.A. Musicians Union and asked for the names of agents that booked rock 'n' roll bands. I was given the name of an agency called Universal Attractions in Hollywood. I liked the sound of that name. Universal Attractions sounded "big time," so I gave them a call and spoke with an agent who seemed interested in The Bonnevilles and said he'd try to find us gigs in L.A. Although Larry remained our bandleader, the California move was my idea and therefore my responsibility. Little did I realize that Universal Attractions was a black agency and specialized in booking famous black artists like Etta James and James Brown. The Bonnevilles would be their first and only white group, an unknown band from Wisconsin with no hit records. Nevertheless, they agreed to listen to our group after we reached L.A.

We drove straight through to Southern California on legendary Route 66. This time, Paul and I took turns driving while one of us slept in the back seat. By the time we reached Gallup, New Mexico, we ran out of money and were almost out of gas. I made a collect call to my grandfather, who wired me twenty dollars via Western Union. When we went to pick up the moneygram, there were several Navajo Indians sitting outside the Western Union office. Wearing blue jeans, T-shirts, and black cowboy hats, popped up like domes on top with a few feathers in their hatbands, the Indians looked mean and angry. They glared at us with contempt. In my heart of hearts, I couldn't blame them. We were in *their* land, *their* "country." We gassed up Paul's car, tried to eat almost raw buffalo-burgers at a roadside stand, and crossed the seemingly endless Mojave Desert, hoping for "happier hunting grounds" in California.

Chapter 6

Johnny "Guitar" Watson, The Olympics

The Bonnevilles arrived at my grandparents' home in Santa Ana, California, in the summer of 1962. I was so young and proud that I never considered what impact our long-term visit might have on their lives. Amplifiers, guitars, my electric piano, and Paul's drums were assembled in the living room. Band members were sleeping on beds and sofas. We had no money, and my grandparents had to support us on their meager Social Security income. We had turned their peaceful home into a rock 'n' roll boarding house.

Intellectual, sensitive people are often the most likely to develop emotional illnesses. This was the case with my eighty-year-old grandmother, Co. Her comfortable, predictable life was replaced with chaos and worry. After several weeks, she drifted into a state of severe depression. Would we ever find work? How could she and Grandpa afford to buy our food? She was overwhelmed with worry and confusion. Co's warm and loving eyes no longer reflected her beautiful soul, but became trance-like and dull. My father said she had "the look of death."

In desperation, I drove the streets of Orange County, hitting every bar and nightclub until I managed to get The Bonnevilles an audition at a club in Costa Mesa called The Firehouse. The club owner liked our music and hired us on a weekly basis. With advances from The Firehouse, we immediately relocated to a motel in Newport Beach and gave my grandmother a chance to recover from the turmoil.

The Bonnevilles were popular at The Firehouse, and packed the club most every night. We were a good little band, with Larry's natural charisma and vocal ability, Paul's great drumming, Tom Hahn's solid bass playing, and my keyboards. Our music included a large variety of styles. We played R&B hits like Chuck Berry's "Johnny B. Goode" and Larry Williams's "Bony Moronie," rock 'n' roll numbers like Rick Nelson's "Travelin' Man" and Ray Sharpe's "Linda Lou," instrumentals like Booker T's "Green Onions" and Chicago blues classics like Muddy Waters' "Got My Mojo Working."

We were doing great at The Firehouse and could have stayed almost forever, but we wanted to play Hollywood and become famous! I called Universal Attractions, and within a few days, a black gentleman in an expensive business suit came to the club. He introduced himself as an agent from Universal and wanted to hear us play. After our set, he smiled, said he liked our music, and wanted to book our band.

After several weeks, the agent kept his word. Universal Attractions booked us at the Doll House, a small but prestigious club in Studio City, just north of Hollywood. We quit The Firehouse and moved to a motel on Ventura Boulevard. The owner of the Doll House decided that The Bonnevilles needed help in drawing customers, so he added two blonde dancing girls called "The Twistin' Twins" to our show. They twisted and gyrated around the stage, and distracted from our music.

One night, Phil Everly from the Everly Brothers came to the club. It wasn't unusual for celebrities to frequent nightspots in the Hollywood area, but Everly's presence was a surprise to us. During our break, we joined Phil at his table and asked if he might help us land a record contract. He said he could get us an audition with Warner Brothers Records, but we'd have to have original material. We didn't have any original songs, just our list of tunes by other artists. After the gig, Everly took one of the "Twistin' Twins" to his hotel suite, filled a bathtub with champagne, and joined her for a midnight swim. We never saw him again.

The money we earned at the Doll House didn't last very long. We tried to regain our gig at The Firehouse, but the owners had hired another band and there wouldn't be an opening for several weeks. Soon we found ourselves broke and out of work, with rent due at our motel in Studio City. I carried my electric piano to the manager's office and asked him to hold it as security. We were so hungry that we considered begging on the streets. My food supply dwindled to a half gallon of ice cream that I kept in a community refrigerator, located in a room behind the manager's office. When I went to retrieve the ice cream for dinner, I found the container in the sink. The manager had defrosted the refrigerator, and my last meal had melted to slush. I picked up the dripping box of ice cream and knocked on the manager's door. When he answered, I threw the container on the pavement in front of his feet and yelled, "That was my dinner!" Hunger was driving me insane.

At a point beyond despair, Universal Attractions got us a one-night show in Tulare, California, at the civic center to backup The Olympics and Johnny "Guitar" Watson. Watson was a legend in Southern California, and his recording of "Lonely Nights" was a traditional favorite in L.A. When I was about fifteen or sixteen, I often played that record while standing in front of a full-length mirror, pretending to sing. I wanted to be Johnny "Guitar" Watson! His primitive guitar solo on "Lonely Nights," basically employing only one note with a blues slur at the end, sounded so great that I eventually learned an important lesson: *"It don't matter how many notes you play, it's how you play 'em!"*

The Olympics had national hits with "Hully Gully," "Peanut Butter," and "Big Boy Pete." Their songs used New Orleans-style rhythms, a "push-pull" rocking interaction between piano and drums that can be heard on records like "High Blood Pressure" by Huey "Piano" Smith, and I learned to play "Hully Gully" on piano when I was sixteen. It was also the first song I played for Larry Lynne when I sat in with the original Bonnevilles during my Navy days. With our upcoming gig, I would complete the circle and play "Hully Gully" with the group that made it famous.

We drove to the small town of Tulare, found the civic center and set up our instruments. There was a large stage at one end of the auditorium, complete with grand piano, heavy red curtains, and numerous flags at each corner. VFW flags, American flags, California State flags, ROTC flags; a typical small town display of patriotism.

Behind the closed curtains, we were introduced to members of The Olympics and to my idol, Johnny "Guitar" Watson. They seemed a little apprehensive, probably wondering if four white boys could play rhythm and blues, but when I played the intro to "Hully Gully" on piano, their fears were quickly abated. They knew we could play their songs.

When the show began, we played a few instrumentals before an emcee called Johnny Watson to the stage. His biggest hit, "Lonely Nights," was an easy song to play, with only two chord changes. I'd been singing this song with the Bonnevilles, and our band knew it well. We knew when to make the changes and where to stop for the frequent breaks that made the song unique and special. Johnny was happy with our music, and I was honored to work with him.

After Watson finished his show, The Olympics were called to the stage. I quickly switched from organ to piano, and we began with "Hully Gully." The audience of teenage kids went wild for that song. A cute girl of about sixteen ran up on stage, kissed me, then ran back to the crowd. She must have been acting on a dare from her friends. Just as I'd realized at El Monte Legion Stadium, being on stage with stars made their sidemen "stars" too.

All the suffering, starvation, and misery I'd endured as a young musician was rewarded that night in Tulare. I would never again need to justify my life with half-truths and exaggerations. I'd become an authentic sideman to R&B stars at age nineteen. I used the money from the Tulare gig to reclaim my electric piano from the motel manager.

We'd played a one-night stand with some famous musicians, but we soon returned to poverty without any gigs coming our way. Our efforts to survive in California, let alone become "stars" were in vain. We decided to return to Milwaukee, a city without much competition. I hocked my electric piano for $100 and bought a ticket to Chicago on the cheapest flight I could find. The plane was an old propeller-driven Hughes Constellation, painted blue to cover the TWA insignias. Our first stop was Dallas, and while en route we encountered some serious weather.

Lightning bolts flashed on both sides of the plane as it wavered and bounced through the darkened sky. Someone had left the cockpit door ajar, and from my passenger seat I could see blue smoke coming from the pilot's control panel. Sitting near the front of the plane, I could smell the acrid odor of an electrical fire. Although a stewardess quickly shut the cockpit's door, other passengers must have noticed that something was wrong. An old lady sitting across the aisle blessed herself and began fingering her Rosary. Her lips moved in silent prayer which must have been answered, because our flying junk-heap managed to land in Dallas.

Almost immediately, technicians in white overalls boarded the plane and began repairing the cockpit wiring. We were advised that the plane was safe, but if we waited several hours we could take another flight to Chicago. About twenty passengers, myself included, decided to remain on board. Our plane somehow managed to reach at Chicago's O'Hare Airport, and I took the North Shore train to Milwaukee. I had less than twenty dollars in my wallet, and rented a tiny room at the White Row Apartments on Kilbourn Avenue for eight dollars per week. The room had a pull-down bed, a small stove with cabinets above, and a heating pipe that ran from floor to ceiling. Included were sneaky brown cockroaches that searched for food at night. I remember turning on the lights and attacking them with Aqua Net hairspray. It "froze" them in their tracks! I'd been to California, backed up some famous artists, but couldn't survive there as a musician. Maybe I could survive in Milwaukee, a relatively small city compared to L.A.

With less than ten dollars in my wallet I walked Wisconsin Avenue, looking for a band that would allow me to "sit in." Again, I found myself 2000 miles from home and almost broke. My Wurlitzer electric piano was in a Hollywood pawnshop, never to be retrieved and my Hammond M3 was somewhere on a train headed to Milwaukee. I had no instrument to play, and my only hope was to line up a job for the future. As I walked Wisconsin Avenue, fate must have been guiding my steps. There is no other way to describe what happened next.

Chapter 7

Vaughn Meader, The Holiday House
Harvey Scales, Denny & The Darnells, Tom Fabré, Stan Musial

It was October of 1962 and snow had begun to fall in Milwaukee. As I walked Wisconsin Avenue on a Saturday night, I was careful not to slip on patches of black ice that lurked on the sidewalks. I still didn't have decent clothes and was wearing the same old saggy suit that was given me by a friend of The Bonnevilles a year earlier. My rented tuxedo, fancy shirts, and patent leather shoes were back at the tuxedo shop. I virtually had nothing but an unwavering belief in my music.

When I reached the heart of the city, I heard the sound of a Wurlitzer electric piano coming from a club called The Spa. I entered the club, took a seat, and ordered a Pabst Blue Ribbon beer. A band called Denny and the Darnells was playing on an elevated stage behind the bar and I liked their music. Bandleader Denny King was a good showman who sang and played lead guitar. The band was hot, with solid drums and bass and a powerful sax player named Tom Fabré. Fortunately for me, the piano player wasn't very good, and I knew I could play much better.

When the band took a break, I introduced myself to Denny and asked if I could "sit in" with his band. He agreed, and invited me to play after the intermission. When the band returned to the stage, I took a seat at the electric piano and played Ray Charles' "What'd I Say." The audience applauded, and Denny asked me to play another song. When I played the Barrett Strong hit "Money," with its mean and hypnotic piano riff, Denny smiled and let me play the entire set. In 1962 Milwaukee, white boys who could play black music were rare.

After the set, Denny invited me to a corner booth and offered me a job, but there was a major problem. My organ was still in transit from California and I didn't have an instrument. Denny left the booth to talk with his piano player, and when he returned, he had some startling news: the piano player agreed to let me use his Wurlitzer piano and amplifier, even though I would be replacing him in the band! Poverty and desperation outweighed the guilt I felt for taking the piano player's gig.

Denny asked me to start playing with his band immediately. I didn't have a car, but that was no problem; Denny would drive me to the gigs. I could hardly believe what was happening. There I was, dressed in shabby clothes, no instrument to play, no transportation and yet I had a gig with a well-known band. The next morning, I heard a knock on my apartment door. There stood Denny with a bag of groceries. He knew I was broke and needed help. I have never known anyone more thoughtful and kind than Denny King.

I began playing weekend club dates with Denny and the Darnells, using the borrowed piano. I was paid fifteen to twenty dollars per night and was able to survive. I learned to cook spaghetti on my stove, and sometimes even bought meatball sandwiches from an Italian deli. Since it was impossible to get Mexican food in Milwaukee, Italian food became my mainstay. It wasn't bland like most Midwestern fare, and it was cheap.

After my Hammond organ arrived, I played a television variety show with Denny on WTMJ-TV in Milwaukee. Someone took a snapshot of me wearing my oversized, ugly coat on television. My clothes would have been more appropriate for a comedy act. Football legend Bart Starr was also on the show for an interview. Not being a sports fan, I had never heard of him. Several months later, I was playing at a fancy nightclub in Milwaukee called The Holiday House. The club owner ran to the stage and said, "Stan Musial is here!" I'd never heard of him either, and thought he might be a jazz musician.

I played many gigs with Denny's band at a venue called Muskego Beach Ballroom. It was always crowded with teenage kids, and I enjoyed playing there. I became a crazy show-off with the Hammond, sitting on top of the organ and playing the keys behind my back or turning the organ on its side and playing it like an accordion. Those were the days when guitar players played behind their heads and sax players fell to their knees to "honk" screaming solos, so I decided to "show off" as much as I could with an organ. Sometimes, sax player Tom Fabré would climb on my shoulders and take "piggyback" tenor solos. To put it mildly, we put on one hell of a show!

Meanwhile at the White Row Apartments, I was almost thrown into jail. Early one morning, a maid unlocked the door and entered my room. She was a middle-aged Polish woman, wearing a black dress and a white maid's cap. At the time, I happened to be sleeping with a young woman. When I saw the maid, I yelled, "Get out of my room!" In response, the maid yelled, "You're sleeping with a whore!"

The maid's words sent me into a rage. Barefoot, I put on my pants and went to the hallway, finding a maid a few feet from my door. She was on her knees, scrubbing the dingy linoleum floor. Beside her was a metal bucket of soapy water. I picked up the bucket and poured the water on the maid's head. "That's for calling my girlfriend a whore," I yelled. She began screaming in Polish and took off running, her arms waving in the air.

Knowing that I was in trouble, I ran barefoot in the snow to the manager's office. The manager was a gigantic woman, and probably weighed over five hundred pounds. Her huge arms covered most of the space on her glass-top desk. I told her that a maid had entered my room and called my girlfriend a "whore." I also admitted to pouring a bucket of water on the maid. I was covering my tracks. I ran in the snow, back to my apartment. In the hallway stood a police officer, dressed like a Russian soldier. He asked me what had happened. After I explained the situation, he seemed to understand. However, he had a surprise for me. I had poured the bucket of water on the *wrong* maid! The maid who'd entered my room was somewhere upstairs, peacefully scrubbing away.

Bobby "Blue" Bland was playing in Milwaukee. I loved his singing, and his music was a big influence on my life. Bobby had the best band I'd ever heard, with a powerful horn section and Wayne Bennett on guitar. I never imagined that Wayne and I would eventually work together in New Orleans in the 1980s.

After the show, I noticed two men on stage. A young black man was singing while the other tried to accompany him on piano. The singer had an excellent voice, but the piano player was sloppy and not at all professional. I could tell he wasn't much of a musician, playing wrong chords and hitting bad notes. After hearing Bobby "Blue" Bland, I was in the mood to play. I asked if they'd let me sit in. When I played, the singer smiled like a Cheshire Cat. I was a white boy who could play rhythm and blues! The singer was Harvey Scales, and he offered me a job in his band. I liked the idea of working with a black singer, and accepted.

I started playing one-nighters with Harvey Scales, who went by the name, "Twistin' Harvey." We might have been the first "salt and pepper" band in Wisconsin, and our gigs were booked throughout the state. Harvey gave a tremendous performance. He sang, did flips on the floor, and danced on top of my little Hammond M3. Years later, Harvey would make his dent in the music world by co-writing the hit song "Disco Lady." The record went to number one on both the R&B and pop charts and was certified as the first single in history to win platinum status, selling over two million copies.

After playing with Harvey for several months, I received a call from Tom Fabré, the sax player from Denny and the Darnells. He offered me a gig at Milwaukee's finest nightclub, The Holiday House. The catch was that I would have to play bass notes. The only way to accomplish this was to play a large organ with foot pedals and low notes on the keyboards. It was time for me to graduate to the Hammond B3.

There was a rented Hammond B3 on stage at The Holiday House, and I had only a few days to practice. There were over twice as many keys as my little Hammond spinet, way more "buttons" to click, and a frightening assemblage of wooden foot pedals. I learned some simple bass lines, and managed to survive opening night. As time went by, I overcame my fears and became comfortable with the instrument. I studied records by Jack McDuff, Jimmy McGriff, and Jimmy Smith, and began to develop a blues/jazz style.

We played The Holiday House six nights per week, and I started making steady money. The first thing I bought was a black suit, along with some white shirts, ties, and shoes. I no longer looked like a street pauper, and even managed to buy a brown 1955 Pontiac. It was old, but had a decent motor and a good heater that kept me from freezing to death in Milwaukee.

The Holiday House booked nationally known acts in the supper club while our trio played in the lounge. I got to meet many famous people, such as Wayne Newton, Totie Fields, Barbara McNair, George Kirby, Eddie Peabody, and Kennedy impersonator Vaughn Meader. Meader was a comedian who could duplicate the voice of President Kennedy and had a hit album called *The First Family*. Vaughn and I became friends, and he often sang with our band after his shows. When President Kennedy was assassinated in 1963, Vaughn's career was also a victim. The Kennedy accent was no longer a laughing matter.

I saw Vaughn many years later in 1978, when I was playing with Bonnie Bramlett at the Bottom Line in New York City. We were in the dressing room when the telephone rang. On line was the doorman, asking if we would allow Vaughn to enter the club as our guest. Bonnie made a remark about Meader, something like, "Let him pay his own way." When I explained that Vaughn was an old acquaintance of mine, she agreed to allow him into the club.

When Vaughn entered our dressing room, he noticed me and said, "I remember you! You were the organ player at The Holiday House in Milwaukee." Fifteen years had passed, and I would never have recognized Vaughn. He had long hair, a beard, and no longer looked like J.F.K. Instead, he resembled a poor, homeless soul. A castaway, a ruined man. I felt sorry for him.

In 1962, he was at the top of the entertainment world, often a guest on the Ed Sullivan Show. His *First Family* album was #1 on the charts, and he was one of America's most popular comedians. It was sad and ironic that he needed my help to get into the Bottom Line. Show business can be very cruel. I am reminded of the song, "Nobody wants you when you're down and out," or, as Delaney Bramlett used to sing, "Everybody loves a winner, but when you lose, you lose alone!" At least I gave him the respect he deserved that night in New York City. Vaughn left this world in 2004 at age sixty-eight. He was a good and decent human being. There is no greater epitaph to any life.

Chapter 8

Jimmy Clanton
and the Short-Lived Stardom of The Skunks

After our Holiday House gig, my friend Larry Lynne from the Bonnevilles offered me a job at a popular Milwaukee club called Monreal's. He was forming a new band called the Catalinas. I gladly accepted Larry's offer, and began working six nights per week.

Monreal's had a stage and dance area downstairs plus another room upstairs for big-name stars called "The Sky Room." The owners, Frank and Sal Monreal, booked Jimmy Clanton for the Sky Room and asked us to be his backup band. I was excited about playing with Clanton. As a teenager, I'd heard his #1 R&B record "Just a Dream" on the radio and watched him sing on American Bandstand. Clanton was just eighteen when he wrote and recorded that record in 1958 with the Rockets, and was one of the first white singers to make the New Orleans R&B/rock 'n' roll sound famous. I could relate to the brokenhearted boy with the high voice that cracked over his lost girlfriend. A Louisiana boy, Jimmy Clanton knew how to sing with feeling and soul.

I was sharing an apartment with bass player Dick Nowak, located near the hotel where Clanton was staying in Milwaukee. Frank Monreal called and asked if I would pick Jimmy up and to drive him to the gig. I was more than happy to comply. As I walked out the door, my roommate said, "Rick Allen, Star-Backer!" It kind of stumped me, but I took it as a compliment, no matter what sarcasm my friend might have intended. Clanton was one of my idols.

I dressed in my finest charge-account clothes: an iridescent light blue suit with a black velvet collar, a white-on-white shirt, dark blue tie, and black Italian shoes. I'd spent half an hour combing my hair into a grand Pompadour. I drove my Pontiac to Clanton's hotel imagining the conversation I was going to have with my teen idol. When I arrived at the luxurious Pfister Hotel, the Milwaukee hotel favored by President Kennedy, I took the elevator to Jimmy's floor and knocked on the door. I was nervous about meeting this rock 'n' roll icon.

When Jimmy answered, I was surprised. He was dressed in pajamas and his hair was a mess, but he was very cordial and invited me into his hotel suite. I took a chair, tried to pretend I wasn't nervous, and watched this star prepare for work. Jimmy opened his suitcase and produced a bottle of beer. My first thought was I can't drink any beer with this man, because I'll need to be sober to play his music. My fears were quickly relieved when Jimmy explained he used beer to style his hair. He splashed some on his head and turned on a blow dryer. When he emerged from the bathroom, he looked like his album cover photos. Good-looking, confident, and famous.

I drove Jimmy to the club, trying my best to make a good impression. We hadn't been able to rehearse, and were only given a list of his songs, which I still have today. Let there be no doubt about it: Jimmy Clanton was a rock star before the term was coined. His records sold in the millions and in 2007 he was inducted into the Louisiana Music Hall of Fame.

The club was packed with barely room to walk. After our band played a few opening numbers, we called Jimmy to the stage. He began with several popular songs by other artists, like Larry Williams's "Boney Moronie," but soon switched to his hit records. When he sang "Go Jimmy Go" and "Venus in Blue Jeans," the audience got up to dance. But when he sang "Just a Dream," most of the crowd stood in awe. A star like Jimmy Clanton was rarely seen in Milwaukee.

It was 1964 and The Beatles were conquering America. Larry Lynne and I liked their music and decided our band needed a gimmick. Larry said, "Let's bleach stripes in our hair and call ourselves The Skunks!" I know this sounds crazy, but no crazier than the shaggy-haired band from Britain. Larry had girlfriends who worked in a hair salon. With towels wrapped around our necks, the girls bleached white stripes on the sides of our heads. We became the first band in Milwaukee to grab the Beatle mania. We were weird and we were different. The band featured Larry Lynne on guitar, Tony Kolp on tenor sax, Duane Lunde on drums, and me on Hammond B3. With a name like The Skunks, it would have been easy for people to say that we "stunk!" But our band was too good to merit such grand dis-*stink*-shun!

With this new look and name, we began to pack Monreal's club every night. I called the Milwaukee Journal and arranged a press release. Soon our band was pictured in all local newspapers, and we were thrust into the exciting world of local fame. For some unknown reason, the papers printed my home address, and teenage girls began knocking at my door, asking for autographs. We decided to have some fun in downtown Milwaukee. Wearing black "Skunk Suits" with white furry stripes on the coats, we took a walk into a Gimbels department store. Up the escalator we rode, only to be followed by so many girls that we had to run. It reached the point where we needed to disguise ourselves. Without a doubt, The Skunks were the stars of Milwaukee in 1964.

We cut some demos at Kennedy Studios in Milwaukee and took a train to Chicago. Wearing our Skunk Suits, we entered Vee-Jay Records, the label that released The Beatles' first albums in the States. Despite our appearance, we couldn't get past the receptionist. Our next stop was Chess Records, the famous blues label. Up the stairs we climbed and spoke with the receptionist. Her office was protected by bulletproof glass, and we had to speak through a small, louvered grill. Eventually, she realized we were harmless, and pushed a button that unlocked the door. Once inside, Leonard Chess greeted us.

The Chess brothers were interested in our Skunks gimmick and invited us to a private office. There was a turntable on the desk, and Leonard Chess played our demo of "Farmer John" and "Justine," songs that had been hits in L.A. but were new to the rest of America. Leonard and his brother Phil seemed to like what they heard, and offered to sign us to Chess Records. We were elated! Phil asked his secretary to type up some contracts that we signed without reading a word. In retrospect, the contracts were probably reasonable. However, I was about to make a major mistake.

Phil Chess put a record on the turntable and said with a smile, "Listen to this!" From the way Mr. Chess was smiling, I got the impression that he considered the record funny! The record was a new song called "High Heel Sneakers" by Tommy Tucker. I laughed and said it sounded like shit! I thought the singing and music were amateurish and sloppy. I had no idea that Mr. Chess had produced it himself and that he'd been smiling with pride, not ridicule. I had no idea the song would become a classic, recorded by over 1000 artists, including The Rolling Stones. Mr. Chess gave me a puzzled look but remained silent. I was digging my own grave, and the hole would get deeper.

Oblivious to this blunder, we left Chess Records overjoyed, contracts in hand. We took a bus to the Chicago Loop, bought a gallon of wine and rode back to Milwaukee on the North Shore train. We were so happy that we made friends with all the passengers in our railroad car, and when we reached Milwaukee we were certain of one thing: we were going to be America's answer to The Beatles! Chess had given us a recording date, and we were ready to take on the world. In the meantime, we continued to play at Monreal's and draw large crowds.

There were over one thousand Clark gas stations in the Midwest and Canada. After seeing a picture of The Skunks in the Milwaukee Journal, Mr. Clark asked an assistant to call Larry Lynne, who informed him that Mr. Clark was interested in our band. Larry talked about the call in passing as if it were utterly insignificant. Obviously, Mr. Clark was interested in some sort of financial investment in The Skunks. Larry must have thought, "Who needs a billionaire oilman to back us. We're The Skunks!" Larry never returned Mr. Clark's call.

We had everything going for us. We were young, we were good musicians, and we had a gimmick. Larry Lynne was a charismatic lead singer. He and I also sang two-part harmonies like the Righteous Brothers and we were all nice-looking kids. The girls loved us and the boys respected our music. We weren't as good as The Beatles, but in 1964, we were better than The Rolling Stones, who were making a British effort at recording American rhythm and blues.

Through the clouds of my youthful ignorance, I sometimes managed to see the light of a good idea. I knew there had been hit records in Los Angeles that never left Southern California. A good example is "Louie Louie," originally recorded by L.A. singer Richard Berry. "I'm Leavin' It Up to You" is another. Written and recorded by Don and Dewey (Don Harris and Dewey Terry), the song was a hit in Southern California in the late fifties. When Dale and Grace, a vocal duo from Louisiana, recorded it in 1963, the song went to #1 on the national charts and sold millions of records. My idea was to record another Don and Dewey song entitled "Farmer John." It seemed a perfect match.... "Farmer John" by The Skunks! It was a strong, catchy rock song that would later top the charts of Billboard and Cashbox Magazines and earn a gold record. Unfortunately, a California band had the same idea at exactly the same time.

Chapter 9

Sonny Boy Williamson

Chuck Berry, Chess Records

On an early April morning in 1964, The Skunks, plus bass player Dick Nowak, boarded the North Shore Train from Milwaukee to Chicago. The weather was damp and the sky dreary, but we were filled with sunny expectations. We were on our way to Chess Records for our first major recording session, and there were no doubts in our minds that the outcome would be sensational. We arrived at 2120 South Michigan Avenue, climbed the flight of stairs and once again confronted the receptionist. Seated behind bulletproof glass, she remembered us from our first visit, pressed a buzzer and allowed us to enter.

Muddy Waters had done a session at Chess the previous night and we were asked to wait in a hallway while the studio was cleared of empty beer cans, whiskey bottles, and other debris. There were no chairs in the hallway, so we sat on the floor and leaned against the wall. Soon a light-skinned black man entered the hall, pushing a broom. He was skinny, and wore a Hawaiian shirt and baggy pants. I assumed he was a janitor. He noticed the skunk stripes in our hair and asked who we were. He seemed interested in our band and sat on the floor beside us, took a few sips from our bottle of wine, and indulged in a friendly conversation.

It wasn't until after our session was over and we were riding the train back to Milwaukee that Larry said, "Chuck Berry was a nice guy." I answered, "What are you talking about? I never saw Chuck Berry." Larry responded, "Hey, that guy with the broom in the hallway was Chuck Berry!" I was taken aback. Chuck Berry! I'd been listening to his records for years and loved his music, but hadn't recognized him. He was probably the most famous person I'd ever met, and I didn't know I'd met him! I'd thought he was a janitor! Later I learned that many of the artists at Chess did little odd jobs around the studio, not for money but just to help "around the house."

When we entered the recording studio, I was aware of the awesome history of the room. Most of my blues idols had recorded there: Muddy Waters, Buddy Guy, Sonny Boy Williamson (II), Otis Rush, and Howlin' Wolf. There was no way we could measure up to the music recorded in that studio. We were just four white boys from Milwaukee with stripes in our hair. We tried to relax our nerves with more wine.

Just when we were ready to record our first song, there was another unexpected visitor: a huge man wearing a derby hat and the most outrageous suit of clothes we had ever seen. One pant leg was blue, the other gray. The same was true of his coat, which was half gray, half-dark blue. We thought our Skunks' costumes were wild and unique, but this man's suit was beyond belief. He carried two briefcases, one in each hand. Sitting on a fold-up metal chair, he opened his baggage. The first case contained bottles of whiskey and the second was filled with harmonicas. Phil Chess yelled over the intercom, "Hello, Sonny Boy!" My God, I was already scared. All I needed was the company of Sonny Boy Williamson! I had grown up listening his music. Songs like "Sad to be Lonesome," with its mean "cut your throat if you mess with me" harp solo, and more recently his biggest hit, "Help Me."

One by one, we introduced ourselves, and I asked Sonny Boy to join me at the piano. Countless blues legends had played that piano, including Otis Spann. It was a medium-sized grand, and I was foolish enough to play some fancy licks, trying to show off my chops. Sonny Boy listened for a few seconds before he growled, "That ain't the blues!" I felt as if someone had hit me with an ax. I wanted shrink into oblivion, but I had to make another attempt at gaining his respect. I said, "I'm not a piano player, I play organ" and asked him to join me at the Hammond B3. I was determined to show him I could play the blues!

We left the piano and moved to a Hammond organ in the corner of the room, sitting together on the bench. Other members of our band stood nearby, wondering what would happen next. I played Sonny Boy's hit, "Help Me," which is based on the same riff as Booker T's "Green Onions," and Sonny Boy began to smile. Man, did that smile ease my mind! He grabbed a harmonica and we jammed together on "Help Me," trading solos.

We left the organ, Sonny Boy downed a slug of whiskey and proceeded to give us a show of harmonica magic. He played the harp sideways, played it with his nose, and put the instrument between his teeth and played with no hands. Then he placed a smaller harmonica in his mouth, completely hidden from view, and continued playing great solos.

He was an amazing musician, but as an orator, Sonny Boy's words could cut to the bone. Most music historians and people who knew him agree he meant to shock musicians into playing with their heart and soul. From the way he smiled at my organ playing and his friendliness toward our band, I believe this was true. Sonny Boy wanted the blues to be real. He wanted musicians to "cut the fancy crap" and get back to the Mississippi cotton fields of his youth where the blues began. If you could musically join Sonny Boy on the porch of a one-room shack next to one of those cotton fields and *really* play the blues, you were his friend. Not easy to do, especially for middle-class white boys or even black kids who were born after 1940. To be completely honest, I don't believe there are any younger musicians, black or white, who will ever equal the sound of the original black bluesmen from the Delta. They were our teachers, we merely their students. A simple slide guitar solo by Muddy Waters completely blows away a million notes by any guitarist from my generation. No matter how great younger musicians might play, there's always something missing; that special, indescribable ingredient of authenticity.

Sonny Boy was one of the original blues musicians to come to Chicago from the South, along with other blues gods like Muddy Waters, Howlin' Wolf, Little Walter, Otis Rush, B.B. King, and a generation later, Buddy Guy. They came from a world that few of us can understand. Hard and tough times turned them into tough and hard men, their sensitivity only revealed in their music. Most of the time, they were on guard. Many of our blues legends, including Sonny Boy, carried knives and guns and didn't hesitate to use them. It's been said that, in England, Sonny Boy pulled a knife on Eric Clapton because Clapton asked him about his real name, (Alex "Rice" Miller). Sonny Boy took that question as an insult. His birth name was none of Eric's business.

Sonny Boy told Phil Chess he wanted to play harmonica on our session. We had planned on recording two songs by Don (Harris) and Dewey (Terry), "Farmer John" and the house-rocker "Justine." Suddenly we needed a song for Sonny Boy's harmonica, and I suggested that we replace "Justine" with the Buster Brown classic "Fanny Mae," a perfect song for the harp. We were rehearsing "Fanny Mae" when Leonard Chess's son Marshall entered the room. He had just returned from England and wanted us to record the song with a "Mersey Beat." We had no idea what a Mersey Beat was and wound up with a backward drum travesty, the snare accents on 1 and 3 rather than the usual 2 and 4. Marshall thought this sounded *something* like the Mersey Beat when in fact it sounded more like a truck with a flat tire, thumping down the road. This was the first big mistake at our session, and the rest would be mine. Stupid mistakes made by a twenty-one-year-old kid with no recording experience. Mistakes any record producer could have easily corrected.

After more than fifty years in the recording business, I know what a record producer is supposed to do. He's supposed to bring out the best in his artists, instrumentally and vocally. He's supposed to make sure the instrumental tracks are strong and solid, offer suggestions, and keep cutting tracks until they're close to perfection. When he hears something bad, he's supposed to stop the tape and ask the musicians to try again. Young artists need help in the studio. In fact, even mega-stars like The Rolling Stones need someone in the recording booth to give them advice. It's almost impossible for an artist to be objective while recording.

At Chess Records, Leonard and Phil Chess personally produced all of their artists. The Chess brothers ran a hands-on record business. If they were recording "Wolf" or "Muddy" and heard something they thought could be improved, they'd stop the tape and make suggestions. But instead of Leonard or Phil producing our session, we were handed over to their son, Marshall. He was very young, about the same age as members of our band, and inexperienced in record production. He would later become an excellent producer and president of The Rolling Stones record company, but in early 1964 he was still green on the vine. When we were ready to record, Marshall sat in the control booth and told the engineer to "roll the tape." He didn't stop us when we made mistakes or offer advice when I tried to scream like James Brown. It was as if we were alone in the studio with just a tape recorder.

"'Fanny Mae,' take one," said the engineer over the intercom. We began with the song that featured Sonny Boy on the intro, our drummer using the backwards and incorrect Mersey Beat that Marshall had requested. When we reached the part of the song where a solo was needed, I decided to hog the show and played organ instead of letting Sonny Boy play harmonica. Organ was a bad idea and didn't fit the song. A guitar or sax solo would have been better and for God's sakes, we had one of the best harp players in the world ready to play his brains out. Instead, the great Sonny Boy Williamson was relegated to playing little rhythmic punches while I took a meaningless solo on the Hammond.

We did a better job with "Farmer John," an up-tempo R&B song with a groove similar to Huey "Piano" Smith's "High Blood Pressure" and the Olympics "Hully Gully." The song incorporated a one-to-five bass line with standard blues changes. Larry and I sang two-part harmony, and Tony Kolp took an excellent saxophone solo in the middle of the song. Recently I received a copy of our Chess session from MCA Records, the company that owns the Chess catalog. After fifty years and many record sessions, "Farmer John" still sounds good to me.

When we returned to Milwaukee, we resumed playing at Monreal's club six nights per week. We thought "Farmer John" would soon be played on local radio stations, but we were about to face a serious problem: our drummer and sax player were only twenty years old. Wisconsin law required musicians to be twenty-one to play nightclubs. Someone reported us to the Milwaukee Police, and our band was busted. Milwaukee's most famous band was unemployed. I filed for bankruptcy and went to Federal Court with Skunk stripes in my hair. I lost my furniture, my car, and my Hammond B3 organ. I had no money for rent and moved back with my parents in Ontario, California. All I had were newspaper clippings and an acetate demo of The Skunks.

One day while driving my father's old 1954 Buick, I turned on the car's radio and heard "Farmer John." I was excited until I realized there was something different about the song. It wasn't *our* "Farmer John"! A band called The Premiers had gotten the same idea and recorded the song in Los Angeles. Unlike Chess Records, The Premiers' record company had the wisdom to release the record. It should have been our version, which was much better. My feelings were a combination of shock, anger, and pride. At least it validated my belief in the song. "Farmer John" by The Premiers was a national hit, reaching #19 on the Billboard charts and selling over a million copies.

When I think back to 1964, I realize the failure of The Skunks was actually a positive stroke of destiny. If we had been successful, my future would have been radically different. I could have helped my parents and grandparents financially, but I would have missed the most valuable part of my life. I would never have met Anne, my wife and best friend, who has meant immeasurably more to me than a hit record.

Chapter 10

Watts and South Central Los Angeles

With the help of my father as co-signer, I was able to buy a Hammond B3 in California. The organ salesman was impressed by my playing and suggested I try for a gig at a black club in Pomona called the Jewell Room. I had never played B3 in a black club, and this would be a challenge.

On a Saturday night, I went to the Jewell Room and listened to the band. There was an organ trio on stage, featuring Leon Haywood on Hammond. Leon was an excellent organist, singer, and showman. I knew he was a more experienced musician than I was, but I asked to "sit in" with his band. It's a common courtesy for musicians to allow others to sit in on club gigs. Also, it gives the house musician a chance to take a break. I always allow other organists to sit in on my club gigs but not major concerts, which are highly regimented with all songs, including encores, planned ahead and arranged in such a way as to get the best reaction from an audience.

Over the years, I have played against many jazz organists, who, like Haywood, were older and more experienced. Although some were great musicians, I usually have the ability to let the "God of Hammond" play through my hands. When this happens, I have only a vague idea of what I'm playing. My fingers play a song of their own, and I groan like an animal as the song *almost* plays itself. As a consequence, I usually get a good response from my audience and other musicians as well.

Most B3 music is not *real* jazz to the technically minded, but more accurately "blue jazz." It's a sophisticated interpretation of the blues, mixed with gospel, jazz licks, and emotional expression. When on stage, I use a combination of fast, intricate runs and simple power-house blues riffs. Creative phrasing is of utmost importance. Without good phrasing (pauses), music would become a mishmash of noise. A song played by an idiot full of sound and fury, signifying nothing.

I try to develop hypnotic, repetitious chants that grab the listener and build a song to the point of anticipation. I learned this technique from Jimmy Smith's recording of "Sonny Moon for Two." Like Jimmy, sometimes I hold down a tonic note with my right thumb and play a repetitious and hopefully infectious riff with the fingers of the same hand. I accompany this with a simple but all-important bass line, also repetitive in nature. An organist can build a great deal of tension with this process until it cries out for a climactic conclusion. When the release finally comes, it's a combination of relief and joy, almost like the *coda* of a Bach fugue.

When I sat in at the Jewell Room, I played two Jimmy Smith songs: "Chicken Shack" and "The Sermon." I started with "Chicken Shack" because it's an easy song to play and always a crowd-pleaser. "The Sermon" requires more technical expertise, which tells other musicians, "Hey man, I can play the 'heavy shit' too!" I ended with Lou Donaldson's "Funky Mama," which was very popular at the time and, like "Chicken Shack," a tune that always grabs an audience.

The club owner was impressed that a white boy could play these songs and offered me a job. I was quite a novelty! The owner, a friendly man named Johnny Dunnigan, suggested that I hire a black drummer named Bobby Finch. We got together for a rehearsal, and I could tell that Bobby was a good drummer who played solid back-beats, (second and fourth beats or, on certain jazz tunes, a snare drum "rim shot" on the fourth beat with a steady cymbal ride).

Finch and I played the Jewell Room for several months as a duo. Real B3 players never need (nor want) to hire bass players. The Hammond covers bass parts perfectly well. In fact, organ bass lines are just as important as melody lines. Right hand melody and left hand bass, often combined with foot-pedal accentuation, interact together so well that a bass player would have to be a mind reader to create the same music. It's truly a situation where the left hand *knows* what the right hand is doing. And speaking of "hands," almost all B3 players, with a few exceptions, employ left-hand bass lines, only complimented by foot pedals. This includes the great Jimmy Smith. I know this to be a fact, because I walked behind him and looked at his hands when he was playing at The Light House in Hermosa Beach.

Bobby and I also played black clubs in San Bernardino, Riverside, Ontario, and other towns in the area. After playing a gig near Hemet, we left our instruments on stage, planning to recover them the next day. When I drove to the club to get my organ, I was surprised to find the doors locked and signs on the windows saying the club was closed for unpaid taxes. After searching for a means of entry, I discovered an unlocked bathroom window. I climbed into the club and rolled my Hammond out the front door, which was easily opened from the inside. I didn't have room in my trailer for Bobby's array of drums, so I left them on stage and told him how to retrieve them. The next day, Bobby Finch went to the club and climbed through the bathroom window. As he was loading up his drums, he was surrounded by police cars, arrested and taken to jail in San Bernardino. Many hours passed before he was released for stealing his own drums!

When I decided that my "chops" were hot enough for Los Angeles, I moved from my parents' home to the Blake Hotel on Franklin Avenue in Hollywood. Tom Fabré, my best friend and tenor sax player from Milwaukee, had a room in the same hotel. We played a few gigs in Hollywood but decided on trying something new and dangerous. "Dangerous" because we planned on visiting the jazz/blues clubs in South Central L.A. Black nightclubs where the best jazz and blues musicians played. In Tom's 1957 Mercury convertible, its raggedy top flapping in the wind, we drove to the then-called Negro section of Los Angeles.

Tom and I entered the Night Life Club on South Western Avenue and heard an excellent organ trio. The club was famous, and often featured name artists like Jimmy Smith, Shirley Scott, "Groove" Holmes,

Jimmy McGriff, and "Baby Face" Willette. By the time we hit the Night Life, I'd played many black clubs near Pomona and had gained confidence. I drank a few beers and listened carefully to the organist, a local musician who was no better on B3 than I was. When my courage reached its high point, I walked to the stage and asked if Tom and I could sit in. The organist smiled and invited us to the bandstand. Many of the club's patrons were ready for a good laugh. I remember seeing smiles on their faces. They were probably thinking, "Look at those white boys up there! They're going to make fools of themselves!"

Tom and I opened with Art Blakey's "Moanin'," a rather serious tune, respected by jazz and blues musicians alike. It involves opening phrases with church-like Amen musical answers, followed by short interludes that require seemingly dissonant bass notes. Then the tune goes into blues changes that allow a musician to "take off and fly." Tom was a self-educated jazz musician and played much like John Coltrane. His solos on "Moanin'" soared over the P.A. system and the audience began to pay close attention. When it came my turn to solo, I hit the keys with a combination of intricate runs and powerhouse blues riffs. When we finished playing, we were rewarded with applause and even cheers. Some people rose to their feet, clapping their hands. "White boys" who could *really play*! Novelties? Absolutely!

During the break, we were complimented by nearly everyone in the club, including the organist and members of his band. Drinks were on the house, and the club owner offered us a gig, playing Wednesday and Sunday nights. A big sign was plastered to the outside wall advertising "Rick and Tom." We packed the Night Life Club whenever we played. It took more than being novelties to accomplish this because novelties quickly become stale. We had to be damn good, maybe even better than some of our black counterparts. And we were making money! We went from "eight cent per night" to "ten cent per night" in just a few weeks! (Cent = Dollar in ghetto lingo.)

There was a little barbeque shack near the Night Life Club, and the delicious smell of hickory smoke filled the evening air. I remember the Louisiana hot link sandwiches, served between two pieces of white bread. The links were broiled in a smoky oven and coated with hot sauce, the best "drunk food" I've ever eaten! After living in Louisiana for over thirty years, I still haven't found a Louisiana hot link sandwich. You can't get Canadian bacon in Canada, you can't get "puffy" fish and chips in Scotland, and you can't get Louisiana hot links in Louisiana!

Several club owners came to the Night Life and offered us gigs. One was "Nat the Cat" who owned an after-hours club called the Pink Kitten. Located at 108th and South Broadway in Watts, the club was painted pink and decorated with cartoons of lascivious cats. "Nat the Cat" hired us to play Sunday mornings from 2:30 until 6:00 a.m. I can't imagine a more dangerous corner than 108th and Broadway in Watts, especially at 2:30 in the morning. But once the after-hours customers heard us play, we were accepted and admired. Nobody bothered us, and we got to play with blues great Lowell Fulson who recorded the hit, "Dark Nights," and legendary sax player Clifford Scott of "Honky Tonk" fame. Playing in the heart of Watts was a musical "do or die" education for Tom and me.

One night after playing the Night Life, Tom and I returned to our hotel in Hollywood at about 3:00 a.m. We went to our separate rooms and prepared for sleep. My room was located at the back of the hotel on the ground floor. It was a cheap old hotel, and I heard the sound of footsteps on the walk behind my room. Looking out my window, I saw the silhouette of a man in the moonlight. He was hiding something under the bushes behind the hotel, and I thought he was hiding money. I was excited, since Tom and I were barely existing on the money we earned playing black clubs. I decided that if the hidden money was stolen, I might as well steal it from the thief.

After waiting for several minutes, I sneaked out to the bushes. Reaching in the darkness, I felt the texture of a paper bag. Quickly, I grabbed the bag, re-entered the hotel and knocked on Tom's door. Once inside I told Tom I'd found a hidden treasure behind the hotel. Filled with grand expectations, we opened the paper bag. To our disappointment and bewilderment, we found that the bag contained balloons! Balloons that were small and filled with powder. We were crazy but not stupid and realized it must be some sort of dope. Tom found a knife and opened one of them. It contained light brown powder, and we concluded it was heroin! We pondered what to do with this unwanted dope. If we tried to sell it, we might be caught and sent to jail. If we turned it over to the police, we might be arrested ourselves or attacked by the criminals who owned the drugs. We decided our best course of action was to return the bag to the bushes, when we heard a heavy rap on the door. Tom had played in many dangerous clubs and had a .32 automatic pistol hidden in his saxophone case. He quickly got the gun, hid against the wall and motioned for me to open the door.

I opened the door to find a very angry Mexican. He burst into the room and said in broken English, "Give me back my shit!" At this point, Tom came from behind the door, jammed the gun against the man's head and yelled, "Freeze, mother!" The man staggered to his knees and raised his hands in submission. As Tom kept the gun pointed at his head, the man begged for mercy. He slowly reached into his coat pocket and brought forth a handful of cash.

The money was appetizing, but accepting it might cause the man to seek revenge. We decided to return the heroin. As Tom kept his gun drawn, I held up the paper bag and said in my high school Spanish, "You can have the bag. We don't want your money." At this point, the man began to cry! I vividly remember him saying, "Thank you, *gracias*, thank you! You are good people." He was probably a "mule" or drug runner, working for some mean and serious dealers. If he lost the bag of heroin, he would have been in serious trouble.

I returned to my room and went to sleep, only to be awakened by an explosion. I jumped from my bed and heard a series of gunshots near Tom's room. I pushed my bed against the door to block entry and lay flat on the floor. I thought the Mexican had killed Tom and that I would be next. After almost an hour, I gained the courage to open my door. I went to Tom's room, expecting to find him dead. When I tapped on his door, Tom answered wearing a look of frustration. He said, "Those explosions were firecrackers. Don't you know what day this is? It's the Fourth of July!"

Unaware of our ordeal with the "heroin mule," our friend from Milwaukee, guitarist Vince Megna, had decided to light firecrackers outside our hotel rooms. His timing couldn't have been worse. And yet, upon reflection, I can only laugh at this bizarre incident. Just another crazy event in my life as a musician.

Another event comes to mind involving Tom Fabré's .32 automatic pistol. This time, the location was the Beachfront Lounge in Monterey, California, where we were booked by Hollywood agent Gale McConkey in the summer of 1964. Gale and her son "Mac" had listened to us play at the Night Life Club, and were impressed with our music. They helped us put a band together consisting of Tom and me, a mediocre guitar player named Jerry, and a drummer named Sonny, recently paroled from the Iowa State Penitentiary.

The gig in Monterey was near an Army base, and on Saturday nights the club was filled with drunken soldiers. One of the soldiers made an insulting remark to me, and I proceeded to use the microphone to humiliate and embarrass him. As I had done to an obese heckler in Milwaukee, I pointed to the chubby soldier, called him Humpty Dumpty and played the theme song from the old Laurel and Hardy comedies. I had the audience laughing at the soldier, and during our break, he sought his revenge. He approached me, shoved me and ripped the front of my coat. He said he would "see me" after the club closed at 2:00 a.m. I told Tom I needed his gun. During the break, we drove to the cottage where we were staying and got the pistol. We were late returning to the gig and the club owner was livid.

The club had a special bandstand. It was semi-circular and had motor-controlled curtains. They were hooked to a metal frame attached to the ceiling. There was a small box on the floor of the bandstand with buttons to open and close them. At the beginning of each set, we would open the curtains and after each set, we would dramatically close them, like a mini stage show in Vegas.

When we returned to the club, the angry soldier was gone, which was fine with me. Tom and I squeezed our way behind the curtains and stepped to the bandstand. Immediately Sonny, our drummer and ex-convict from Iowa, attacked Tom. Sonny was a big man, and Tom was no match for him. He grabbed Tom by the neck and said, "You're late, and I've been catching hell from the club owner!" Sonny was like a wild man, yelling at Tom and choking him in a bizarre outburst of rage. Tom was my best friend, and I told Sonny to leave him alone. Sonny paid no attention and continued to push and shake Tom. I decided to take action. I pulled the .32 automatic from my waistband and pointed it at the drummer. Funny how this was happening behind a thin curtain, our unknowing audience on the other side, passively sipping their drinks.

When Sonny saw the gun, he became terrified. Down upon his knees he fell, all his prison bravado gone. I ordered him to sit at his drums. I remember saying, "Sonny, you're bigger and stronger than I am, but I'm crazy! If you ever attack Tom or me, I'll be at the foot of your bed the next morning with this gun!" I was bluffing, but Sonny never bothered us again. I found the box that controlled the curtains, pressed a button and opened the drapes. It was time to rock and roll.

Chapter 11

Carjacked in Watts with my Future Bride

Shortly after returning to Los Angeles, I took a job with The Limits, a popular club band recommended by my agency, McConkey Artists Corporation in Hollywood. I played many gigs in Southern California with The Limits and eventually found myself playing at a resort in Downey called The Tahitian Village. This was a steady job, which lasted many months. The clientele consisted of wealthy businessmen and their wives, even NASA astronauts. I remember meeting Wally Sheraw and Buzz Aldrin at the bar, where they bought me a beer.

In the summer of 1965, Watts was a blazing inferno. The Tahitian Village, located in the mostly white suburbs, was about eight miles from the ever-increasing riot zone. The ugly red glow of fire dominated the night sky. Police sharpshooters were stationed on the roof of The Tahitian Village while Jeeps carrying armed National Guard soldiers patrolled the streets. At the same time, I was on stage with The Limits playing "Wooly Bully" and "Mustang Sally" like Nero playing his fiddle while Rome burned.

I was twenty-two years old and had met many girls since I began playing nightclubs. While most were one-night stands and quickly forgotten, some of the girls were high class, refined and potential wife material. But after a heart-crushing breakup with my high school sweetheart, a breakup so painful that I joined the Navy in a futile attempt to forget, I was reluctant to fully trust another woman. For over five years, I wouldn't allow myself to fall in love. It was a matter of self-preservation. I couldn't risk another heartbreak. All of this was about to change because of a hamburger.

Late one morning, I was awakened by a persistent knock on my hotel door. Peering through the peephole, I saw the face of a pretty woman. When I opened the door, she smiled at me and said she had brought my breakfast, a cheeseburger on a tray. I recognized her as Anne, a girl I'd met at the Tahitian Village the previous night. I invited her into my room, and when she sat on my sofa I was struck by her beauty. Her eyes were mystic blue, her auburn hair stylish, and her voice a happy song. More importantly, as we engaged in conversation, I found her to be highly intelligent, sensitive, and open-minded. She had filed for divorce from an unhappy teenage marriage while I was recovering from five years of self-imposed exile at "Heartbreak Hotel." Anne and I developed a friendship that soon turned to love. It was time for me to trust another girl. Anne was worth the risk of another heartbreak.

Several weeks after the Watts riot smoldered to a bad memory, I made one of the biggest mistakes of my life. I decided to take Anne to "Nat the Cat's" Pink Kitten club where I'd played in Watts in 1964. I was eager to sit-in on organ. I drove Anne's red 1965 Mustang to 108th and South Broadway, passing many burned-out buildings and stores with plywood covering their windows. I thought we'd be perfectly safe at the Pink Kitten because Nat the Cat would remember me. This decision almost cost us our lives.

The Pink Kitten club was gone. It had been burned to the ground and was just a pile of rubble. I made a U-turn in the Mustang and drove a few blocks in search of a music club that was still in business. To my left, I saw the neon lights of a small nightclub and heard the sounds of a live band. The club looked like a decent place, so I made another U-turn and parked the little car near the front door. Anne had never been to a black club before, but I assured her all would be fine, once the people heard me play.

When we entered the club, the first thing I noticed was a Hammond organ on the bandstand. Without an organ, we'd have tried to find another club. I also noticed that its cover lid was closed. All eyes were upon us when we walked into the club, a white boy and his girlfriend in Watts, especially so soon after the riots. But I knew that after I sat-in on organ, we'd be welcomed with open arms. A waitress seated us in front of the bandstand where a trio was playing, made up of sax, bass, and drums. When the band took a break, I told the sax player that I played Hammond and wanted to sit in. He said that would be fine with him, but it was the organist's night off, and he always locked the organ when we wasn't playing. The sax player said he couldn't unlock the Hammond without a special key, and he drifted to the bar for a drink.

As we were about to leave, three men approached our table. Introducing themselves as fellow musicians and friends of the band, they bought us several rounds of drinks. Strong whiskey drinks, that neither Anne nor I were used to drinking. One of them said, "Say man, could you do us a favor? We need a ride home." They seemed to be nice people, so I agreed. We staggered outside the club and climbed into Anne's Mustang, which seated four people comfortably but wasn't designed to seat five. As a result, Anne sat on the middle-hump so that one of our new "friends" could squeeze in next to her. The other two men sat in the back.

We drove several blocks until we saw the lights of another nightclub. One of our passengers asked me to drop him off at the club because he wasn't ready to go home. After he climbed from the Mustang, he motioned to me from the sidewalk. He whispered, "Watch out for those people! They're out to get you!" I didn't believe him. I thought he was just drunk and paranoid. I foolishly believed that the other men were musicians, and to this day I still trust *real* musicians, no matter where they're from or what race they might be. It's sort of a universal brotherhood. I returned to the car.

I don't remember their names, so I'll refer to them as "front-seat man" and "back-seat man." I drove south on Broadway, with Anne still squeezed between the front-seat man and me. The front-seat man said he needed to sit where he could give me directions. After several miles, he asked me to turn onto a residential street and pointed to a small home with a long driveway. I pulled up the drive and waited for our friends to depart. Instead, they remained seated and quiet. A feeling of fear and suspicion suddenly came over me. My intuition flashed, "Get out of here!"

I jammed the car into reverse, floored the gas and backed out the driveway, sideswiping a picket fence. I righted the twisting car on the street and raced to a nearby gas station that was still open for business.

The front-seat man said, "What's the matter, bro? We just want a ride home!" I was drunk from the whiskey and felt I'd insulted our companions. I still believed they were musicians and could be trusted. Following the front-seat man's directions, I drove a few blocks before turning onto another side street. The front-seat man pointed to a small stucco house and said it was his home. The street was dark and empty. I pulled up the driveway but left the motor running, again expecting our passengers to leave. Almost immediately, the front-seat man ripped the keys from the ignition and attacked Anne. Being a full-blooded Scot with the courage of her distant cousin, Sir William Wallace, she clawed his face like a wildcat. It happened so fast that before I had a chance to react, he jumped from the car and ran up the driveway in pain.

I realized that this was my chance to use some psychology on the back-seat man, who was sitting directly behind me and could have strangled me at any moment. It was definitely a matter of brain over brawn. I said, "Hey man, I'm not just a 'fay dude. I'm a brother. I've played all over South Central L.A. You've got to help us!" Hearing the commotion, the homeowner turned on a yellow porch light and I realized that we were parked in an innocent stranger's driveway.

The front-seat man returned to the car, threw me the keys and ordered me to drive. He put his hand into his coat pocket and said he had a gun. My own Scots-Irish blood surfaced, and I was boiling mad! I pushed the gas pedal to the floor and said, "Go ahead and shoot! Go ahead and kill us. Both of you bastards are going to die too! I'll crash this car into a telephone pole." Our captors became the captured. Racing down a wide street full throttle, I had them under my control. I drove over 100 mph, going through every red light, hoping for the police. Not one cop was in sight. As fate might dictate, the road narrowed and became a dead end. I jammed on the brakes, almost hitting a barricade. Again, the front-seat man tore the keys from the ignition and resumed his attack upon Anne. I climbed out of the car, and the back-seat man decided to run. He yelled, "Hey!" and tossed me the car keys, which landed in the street. I picked them up and turned to see Anne fighting in the front seat.

I opened the passenger door and pulled Anne's attacker from the car.

I was so angry that I gave him a bolo punch to the face. He took off running down an alley, carrying Anne's purse. I chased him, filled with rage. When I cornered the man he said, "What do you want? The purse?" I didn't want the purse; I wanted to kill! I grabbed him by the neck and tried to strangle him, but I was no match for the strong black man. He threw me down upon a pile of lumber in someone's backyard and was about to hit me with a 2x4 when the back-seat man came to my rescue. He grabbed the 2x4 from his friend, and they both took off running into the night. We were lucky. Our kidnappers knew we could identify them. Under California law in 1965, anyone convicted of kidnapping and attempted rape could be sentenced to death in San Quentin's gas chamber. Killing us would have been the logical alternative.

Anne was a Scottish lassie, both of her parents born in the land of heather, and I was from an old Colonial-American family of British descent. Not that ethnic origin was of great importance, but it helped us form a bond. We'd both grown up hearing our parents' records of the same Scottish music, tunes like "Annie Laurie" and "Loch Lomond" and songs by Scottish comedian Sir Harry Lauder. We also agreed on religion (or rather non-religion), politics, music, and a basic philosophy of life that centered upon non-conformity and a search for happiness. From that "Day of the Hamburger," Anne has never left my heart. I won't use the worn-out term "soul-mate" because clichés tend to trivialize. I can only say that the mystical magic of love came upon us as if already written in our book of life. Six months after we met, we exchanged wedding rings in Hawaii where I had a gig in Waikiki. Anne had two children from her first marriage, an eight-year-old son named Craig and a six-year-old daughter, Kelli. To my happy surprise, the children said they wanted me to be their dad. I did my best to help raise them, and we're very close to this day.

Anne has been my partner and most ardent music-supporter for almost five decades. Never did she allow me to give up my music, even when we lived in poverty. Not even when I offered to attend law school at the University of Southern California. I can still hear her saying, "I didn't marry a lawyer; I married a musician!"

Chapter 12

Richard "Groove" Holmes, Jimmy McGriff & "Baby Face" Willette

Despite our brush with death in Watts, I never changed my attitude toward black people. I had simply been a fool for trusting strangers. Several months later, I decided to take Anne to the Night Life Club in South Central L.A.

There was a world of difference between the Night Life Club in South Central and the Pink Kitten in Watts. The Night Life was a high-class jazz club, and even though it was located in the black section of town, it was many miles to the north of Watts, almost in downtown Los Angeles. It was a more affluent area, where people lived in decent homes, had good jobs, and drove nice cars. When we entered the Night Life, the bartenders and owner remembered me and welcomed us with hand slaps and free drinks.

Organist "Baby Face" Willette, wearing a black patch over one eye like a pirate, was on stage with his trio. Although I'd never heard of him, he was a good musician and I enjoyed his playing. After Willette finished a song, I walked to the stage and asked if I could sit in. He agreed and let me take his place at the Hammond. Before I climbed on stage, he politely asked if he could sit in our booth with Anne so she wouldn't be alone and targeted by men "on the make." I thought that would be a good idea, and thanked him.

I played two or three songs by Jimmy Smith and finished the set, receiving a warm response from the audience. I knew my playing was at least equal to Willette's. I left the stage and joined Anne and Baby Face at our table. He smiled and asked if he could give me some advice. He leaned close to my ear and said, "You play great, man. You have fantastic chops; better than mine. But you're giving it all away too soon! You need to hold back. Let the song build and tease the audience, then hit them with everything you've got!" I wasn't the least bit insulted by Willette's remarks. He was older and wiser, and I knew he was right. I should have remembered this lesson from my first demo session in Milwaukee, when I recorded (and destroyed) my organ solo by playing too many notes, but it took Willette to hammer this message into my head. Willette was a real gentleman whose only intention was to help me become a better musician.

Baby Face told us that B3 monster Richard "Groove" Holmes was playing up the street at the Tiki Island Club. We thanked Willette, shook hands, and headed for the Tiki. The owner was a dignified lady called Miss Marjorie. She'd heard me play at the Night Life the previous year and welcomed us with hugs and kisses. Miss Marjorie escorted us to a table and bought us a round of drinks. As usual, I chose beer while Anne requested white wine.

"Groove" Holmes was playing a Hammond on stage. A bear of a man, he was on the same musical level as Jimmy Smith but with a style all his own. I would never have asked to sit in after such an extraordinary organist. "Groove" was a thirty-three-year-old master musician, while I was just a twenty-two-year-old kid, still learning. In a few moments, I'd wish we'd never entered the club.

After Holmes finished his set, Miss Marjorie walked up to the stage. To my horror, she grabbed a microphone and said, "We have a special guest here tonight. Give a big hand for Rick Allen! He's going to play for you!" .

I was scared to death, and upset that Marjorie would force me into such a terrible situation. Only a fool would have dared to sit in after "Groove" Holmes! But the organ bench was empty, the band and audience waiting. I had no choice but to play. I walked up to the organ, sat down and played "Sunny Moon for Two" by Jimmy Smith. I didn't try to compete with Holmes by playing anything close to his style because that would have been musical suicide. After I finished, the audience gave me a reasonable amount of applause, and I returned to my table with Anne. I was relieved that my trial by fire was over but couldn't help wondering what "Groove" thought of my playing. My question would soon be answered.

During intermission, a waitress approached our table and said, "Mr. Holmes would like to buy you both a drink." I was astonished. I ordered a glass of wine for Anne and another beer for myself. After a few minutes, "Groove" came to our table and politely asked for a chair. When he sat down, he was kind enough to compliment my playing. It was an honor for any organist to be complimented by Richard "Groove" Holmes and the memory of that night will always be with me. However, I was in for another surprise. Miss Marjorie came to our table and asked, "Rick, would you like to be our 'Celebrity of the Week'? We'll advertise your name on the radio!" To be "Celebrity of the Week" at a club where "Groove" Holmes played was an honor I couldn't refuse.

I remember listening to KGFJ, the major black radio station in Los Angeles and hearing my name mentioned as "Tiki Island's Celebrity of the Week." Anne and I drove to the club on "Celebrity Night" and saw my name on the marquee. I felt nervous about the celebrity thing. I was a good organist, but certainly not a celebrity. We stopped at a corner bar for a shot of Scotch to calm my nerves. Anne told me not to worry, that all would be well. Gaining courage, we drove back to the Tiki Island and parked the red Mustang. Walking into the club, we were greeted by Miss Marjorie, who quickly seated us and sent free drinks to our table. I immediately switched from Scotch to beer.

There was a middle-aged organist on stage, and I found his playing boring and weak. Musically, he wasn't saying anything on the organ. No feel, no "groove," no power. Nothing to make the audience smile and say, "Yeah!" In addition to all this, he later proved to be rude and tried to sabotage my performance.

When Miss Marjorie announced my name, the organ player left the stage, taking his drummer with him! Drummers usually remain on stage to accompany organists, and I was shocked. It's extremely difficult for me to play without a drummer, because I fly in many directions tempo-wise and need to hear a steady rhythm to keep me grounded. Unlike the piano, the organ is not a rhythm instrument. Leaving me without a drummer was an intentional slight. The house organist wanted my performance to fail.

When I took a seat at the Hammond, I noticed that the settings were completely wrong for jazz and blues. I quickly changed the settings to those of Jimmy Smith and other *real* organ players. Next, I realized that the Leslie speaker was set at low volume, as if the other organist was afraid of the B3 and didn't want to be noticed. He wanted to "hide" his own incompetence. I reached behind the Leslie, found the volume knob and turned it up, full blast!

Without a drummer, I decided that "Summertime" might win the audience. I started with a slow treble riff between three high notes (G, Bb, C) and drove them faster and faster until they became a blur of sound, followed by a minor seventh blue-note run down to the lowest tones on the keyboard. Then, switching to 6/8 time, I started to slowly play my way back up the keys, using the same blue-notes (C, Eb, F, G, Bb, C), playing each note faster than the previous until I reached a high-treble trill between Bb and C. Then I stopped and hit the first familiar notes, "*Sum-mer*," and only when I hit the high C note for "*Time*" did the song actually begin. This intro was strong, and people shouted and whistled when it resolved into the familiar melody.

When I reached the *coda*, I used every trick of crowd-pleasing showmanship I knew. Holding down the dominate G pedal with my left foot, my right hand climbed the chromatic scale with trills until I reached high C. Then I played a very strong full-organ F-minor chord with the Leslie speaker spinning fast, resolving to a C-minor chord, which was a typical, although minor, church "Amen." I sustained the chord for a few seconds, letting it resonate through the nightclub. Then I stopped. "Summertime" was over. My fate was up to the jury.

For a moment, the audience was silent and I thought I might have failed. Then people started clapping and began to stand up. They were rising from their chairs! Anne and Miss Marjorie were standing with them, clapping and smiling. As we left the club, we walked past the other organist who was smoking a joint on the sidewalk. I gave him a smile and shook my head in disgust.

The night was still young, and I was "feeling my oats" after my victory at the Tiki Island. Anne and I decided to drive to Hermosa Beach, where the great organist Jimmy McGriff was playing at The Lighthouse, a racially-mixed jazz club. McGriff was a star and his recordings of "I've Got a Woman" and "All About My Girl" were hits that crossed racial boundaries on radio stations nationwide. He inspired many organ players, myself included, with his straight-ahead blues style of playing. Jimmy opened the door for many B3 players all over America by popularizing the Hammond. He was one of my most influential teachers (via his records), and I still use many of his ideas today.

When we reached The Lighthouse, we found a table close to the stage and listened to Jimmy's incredible music. Somehow, I mustered the courage to walk up to the bandstand and ask Jimmy if he'd allow me to sit in. I'd managed to survive "Groove" Holmes a few weeks earlier and figured I might as well try again with another famous organist. Jimmy said, "Sure, man, I'll let you play the last song of my set." True to his word, McGriff motioned for me to come up to the bandstand while his sax player and drummer remained on stage to back me up.

I decided to play Jimmy Smith's "Sonny Moon For Two," with its infectious groove and blues changes that gave me room to employ lots of improvisation. The audience applauded when I finished the song, but I was well aware they'd rather have been hearing McGriff. Sadly, Jimmy felt otherwise. He took a seat at our table and said, "After that song, I don't know what to play. I can't top that!" I felt embarrassed and guilty. Many times, musicians use the stage as a battlefield to destroy each other, but I never intended a contest with Jimmy McGriff. I just wanted to play my best and make a good impression. He was the star. The audience came to hear him play, and they liked his music more than mine. In fact, I liked his music better than my own! I wish Jimmy had realized this at The Lighthouse.

After Jimmy left our table, a man in a business suit approached me and introduced himself as "Dootsie" Williams, the owner of an independent record label called DooTone Records. Mr. Williams liked my playing and offered me a recording contract. He gave me his card, but I never called his office. I thought I was too good for a small label and wanted to sign with a major label like Blue Note or Columbia. Years later I learned that Dootsie Williams had produced many records, including the mega-hit "Earth Angel" by The Penguins, probably the most enduring and popular doo-wop song of all time.

Ignoring Mr. Williams might have been one of my biggest mistakes in music. If I had called and talked to him, he could have helped me build a career as a soloist playing blue/jazz organ. Because of this missed opportunity, I drifted away from the world of jazz and into rhythm & blues and rock. My next stop would be Hollywood. Instead of being a featured instrumentalist, I would spend most of my life as a sideman and later, a studio musician. I'm not sure which road would have been better.

Chapter 13

The Sunset Strip

Al and the Originals, Richard Pryor, Timi Yuro,
Darren McGavin, Edmond O'Brien

Al and the Originals was the best band in Los Angeles. At least, that
was my opinion at age twenty-two. I'd taken Anne to hear them many
times and was excited when they offered me a job. For several months
I'd been idle, other than a short stint with a band called The Critters at
the 49er club in El Monte. Formerly a country-western bar, the 49er
had switched to rock music. While the gig didn't seem important at
the time, it was at the 49er that Al Navarro from Al and the Originals
first heard me play and decided to hire me, replacing Dennis Provisor
on keyboards. Dennis was a good singer and showman but he played a
little Farfisa organ. Most Hammond players hated Farfisas because of
their "cheesy" sound. We had little respect for the Farfisa. Compared
to a Hammond B3, the Farfisa was a child's toy.

Al and the Originals was a racially-mixed band with three blacks, a
Chicano, and me. On guitar was Arthur Adams, a genius musician
who would eventually record with James Brown, Ray Charles, and
Quincy Jones. On drums was a young man called Ron Ringo, who

had a great microphone personality. Al Navarro was the bandleader and played bass, but the most important member of the band was a black Creole from Louisiana named Bobby Angelle.

Most bands, including The Beatles, start out in clubs. Not formal clubs with tuxedo-clad waiters, but cellar clubs and bars. While dreaming of fame and fortune, musicians play clubs for money and learn to perform for live audiences. The most important clubs in L.A. were on the Sunset Strip. Frequented by the Hollywood elite, those clubs offered the possibility of being discovered by producers, talent scouts, and agents.

Al and the Originals were playing at The Galaxy on Sunset Boulevard, almost next door to the Whisky a Go Go. Specializing in the rhythm and blues, our band covered most of Motown's hits as well as records by Otis Redding, Wilson Pickett, James Brown, and other R&B artists. What kept us from success in the record business was that we had too many stars, each with his own agenda. There was no group ambition. Arthur Adams, Bobby Angelle, and even drummer Ron Ringo wanted to pursue their solo careers. Al and the Originals was just a bread-and-butter band to them, a way to pay the bills. As a consequence, Adams became a studio musician, Angelle had a regional hit with "Love the Way You Love," and Ron cut a record that went nowhere. None of us would ever achieve separately what we might have achieved together.

Bobby Angelle, a former protégé of Little Richard's, was such a good singer and showman that he epitomized the word "great." Far ahead of his time in 1966, he wore a different outfit for each set. His costumes, designed by his girlfriend Geraldine, glittered with gold and silver. His hair was styled in a fancy "do" and he wore eye makeup. His voice was amazing. He could sing like anyone, from Smokey Robinson to James Brown, Aaron Neville to Ray Charles, and also had a unique style of his own. After all my years in the music business, I still rate Bobby Angelle as the best singer I've ever worked with and one of the best I've ever heard. Just to be on stage with him was an honor.

In the mid-1960s to the early 1970s, the Whisky a Go Go was the most famous nightclub in the world. The launching pad for superstars like Jimi Hendrix, The Who, Cream, The Byrds, and Led Zeppelin, some bands actually *paid* the Whisky to play the club for exposure. Our band was so popular that we gave the Whisky competition. Lines of people coming to hear us at the Galaxy literally stretched around the block. Our fans covered the sidewalk on Sunset Boulevard, past the Hamburger Hamlet and up a side street toward the Hollywood Hills. Once there was even an armed robbery in our line of customers. That's a long line!

Occasionally we had visitors from bands playing the Whisky. I remember the Young Rascals and also The Doors coming to the Galaxy during their breaks. None of them dared to sing after Bobby Angelle except for a girl named Timi Yuro. She joined us on stage and sang her hit song, "Hurt." Her voice was so great and powerful that she held the microphone at arm's length. Timi was the only singer willing to share the stage with Angelle on the Sunset Strip.

It was at the Galaxy that I met Joey Vieira, who co-starred in the original *Lassie* TV series, playing young Jeff's (Tommy Rettig) best friend, "Porky." Joey was "Hollywood to the bone." His father, George Vieira, was assistant director for such classic films as Jimmy Stewart's *Spirit of St. Louis* and Susan Hayward's *I Want to Live*. Joey's aunt was 1930's Broadway and Hollywood screen star Ruby Keeler, married to the great Al Jolson. His half-brother, Kenny Weatherwax, co-starred on *The Addams Family* TV series, playing the part of Pugsley, the chubby little kid in the Addams' spooky house. In the year 2000, Joey landed a supporting role with Mel Gibson in the epic film, *The Patriot*, playing Peter Howard, the hard-of-hearing, peg-legged father whose daughter marries Gibson's son, played by Heath Ledger. Because of his background Joey had many connections, including being a business partner in both The Hullabaloo Theater in Hollywood and Sound City Recording Studios in Van Nuys.

Joey arranged for our band to play at The Hullabaloo, formerly called the Moulin Rouge and home of the TV show, *Queen for a Day*. Later it would become the Aquarius Theater, showplace for the rock operas *Jesus Christ Superstar,* and *Hair*. The Hullabaloo was one of the most important venues in Hollywood. Its stage had been graced by countless performers, from Liberace to Jimi Hendrix.

I love to play theaters like The Hullabaloo. It's a thrill to see the scuffed floorboards, the dark red curtains, the ropes, the footlights. I can still smell the dusty odor of the curtains and remember the excitement of peeking at the audience from the corner of the stage. Some of the greatest highs of my life have come from playing theaters. There is a special feeling they generate, a feeling unequaled by college auditoriums or even arenas like Madison Square Garden. No matter the size of the audience, no matter the intensity of the spotlights, there is nothing like hearing a stage hand yell, "Curtain going up!" That's the real thing. That's your dream. That's what you live for. As Irving Berlin wrote in 1954, "There's no business like show business!"

Behind the gigantic curtains, The Hullabaloo boasted the first revolving circular stage in America. Sixty feet in diameter with a backdrop curtain in the center, the stage was designed to allow one act to prepare while another performed. We arranged our equipment on the hidden side of the stage, and when it came our time to play, the stage began to move. We felt the floorboards vibrate and the gears grind as the stage rotated like a merry-go-round, placing us in position behind the main curtain. Above the murmuring crowd, the announcer said, "Ladies and Gentlemen, Al and the Originals!" The curtain rose, and the lights reached an almost blinding level. Angelle walked to center stage, fell to his knees and sang "Please Please" by James Brown. From that point on, we had the audience in the collective "palm of our hands." All I had to do was back up Bobby Angelle and Arthur Adams and let them carry the show. With their mutual talent, our first engagement was easy and fun and our performance a resounding success. The audience went wild with applause.

The management wanted to book us for another engagement, but Joey had a different idea. He decided that our next performance would not feature Angelle and Arthur. Instead, it would feature only three musicians: Me, Myself, and I. No band, no drummer, no nothing except me and my Hammond B3. I remembered playing the Tiki Island club without a drummer before an audience of about fifty people. Joey expected me to do the same in front of two thousand!

At first, I emphatically refused to participate in Joey's plan. Not only was I terrified to play alone, I thought the idea was ridiculous. But Joey was an extremely powerful salesman and somehow convinced me that I had the ability to "grab the crowd" and build my reputation in Hollywood. I begrudgingly succumbed to his wishes. Like some of my bandmates with their own agendas, Joey saw Al and the Originals as a springboard to my individual stardom. I didn't share this view, and didn't want "individual stardom." All I wanted was to be part of a successful band that could top the charts with hit records.

All too soon, the night of my solo engagement at The Hullabaloo arrived and the stage began to revolve. Around went the ride until my B3 and I reached the main curtains. I could hear the murmur of the audience as I awaited my impending doom. The announcer said, "Ladies and gentlemen, Rick Allen on Hammond organ!" Up went the red curtain and on came the lights, so bright that I could hardly see the audience. I was terrified. My foot on the organ's volume pedal began to tremble and shake. My fingers were almost frozen with fear. For the first time in my life, I experienced genuine stage fright. As Stephen Stills would later say at Woodstock, I was "scared shitless."

I closed my eyes and began to play "Summertime." I built the song in the same way I'd done at the Tiki Island. I was so scared that I never really got into the groove, but somehow managed to finish the piece. After I played the last chord, I began to hear the oceanic roar of a large audience. It was like the sound of heavy rain on a rooftop. I tried to see the crowd through the stage lights, but all I saw were shadow images. Images of people standing! I looked harder. The whole theater was standing. My face ran with tears as the curtain closed. Tears of relief, happiness, and sorrow. Relief that the show was over, happiness that Joey and Anne were proud, and a touch of sorrow that my father hadn't lived to see me receive a standing ovation in Hollywood. It would have dispelled any doubts he harbored about my ability as a musician. A young Richard Pryor was seated next to Joey in the audience. After my performance, he told Joey, "Man, I can't believe that guy's white. He plays like a brother!" It still makes me happy to know that a man of Richard Pryor's talent enjoyed my music.

I continued playing with Al and the Originals at the Galaxy on a weekly basis. One night, a producer from Universal Pictures came to the club and decided to use both The Galaxy and our band in a two-hour pilot for a TV series called *The Outsider*, starring Darren McGavin, Ann Sothern, and Edmond O'Brien. Suddenly we were thrust into the world of Hollywood movies. Our egos, at least mine, were inflated to the point of explosion!

We arrived at Universal Studios at 6:00 a.m. and were greeted by an assistant director, who sent us to wardrobe for off-white shirts; our white shirts were too bright for Technicolor film. If I'd ever felt like a star, it was at Universal. Thoughts of my father's days as an extra for Charlie Chaplin flashed through my mind as if to say, "Look, Dad, I can make movies too!"

We were assigned a trailer near the soundstage, then stood in line until a makeup artist covered our faces with Max Factor. My makeup was very white and made me look like a ghost. I don't remember what they did with our black musicians, but surely they didn't paint their faces white! We returned to our trailer and drank some coffee. A Universal Studios tour had begun, and when we walked outside the trailer, tourists flocked to take pictures. To "Ma and Pa Kettle from Ypsilanti," we were movie stars.

When it was time to begin filming, we entered the soundstage designed to look like the interior of the Galaxy club. The director yelled "action," and music from a song we'd recorded the previous night filled the room. We had to pantomime our music, which became tiresome. For over twelve hours, we pretended to play our instruments while the director took various shots and corrected actors with suggestions. Movie-making was so repetitive that it became boring. After about five hours of shooting, we were allowed a break for lunch.

Feeling like a genuine movie star, I stepped outside to face the tourists. Click-click went their cameras as I bathed in my own glory. When I returned to the soundstage, I took a seat on a wooden sawhorse and ate a sandwich. When I got up, a nail caught the seat of my pants, tearing open the seam and exposing my boxer shorts. A good lesson for Rick Allen the movie star! I spent the remainder of the day with one hand behind my back, holding shut the rip in my pants. Such was my debut and final bow as an actor. When we watched the movie on TV, I was on screen for less than ten seconds!

Chapter 14

I Return to Whittier with Stars of Doo-Wop

The Coasters, The Penguins, The Isley Brothers,
Jesse Hill, The Shields, Robert & Johnny,
Sonny Knight, Johnny "Guitar" Watson

I'm reminded of the story of Moses, who left Egypt under the worst of circumstances and after many years returned a transformed man. Not that I returned to Whittier with miraculous powers, but in terms of respect from my peers, I came close. When I left Whittier at age seventeen, I was a skinny kid, called "Stork" by my gym teacher, scorned by my girlfriend, disrespected by my parents, and jailed by the Whittier Police for stealing quarters from an ice machine with some friends. Almost six years later, I returned in a Cadillac De Ville, with a beautiful wife and one of the best bands in Southern California.

It was the summer of 1966, and Al and the Originals were rotating gigs between the Galaxy in Hollywood and The Plush Bunny, located on the outskirts of Whittier. The "Bunny" was the most popular nightclub in eastern L.A. and lived up to its name. Plush red carpets and ornate wallpaper, black leather booths, tables with swivel seats, and a classy stage that included a dressing room for the performers. We were hired to play six nights per week from 9:00 P.M until 2:00 A.M.

Los Angeles deejay "Huggy Boy" brought famous artists to The Plush Bunny on Saturday nights, and I got to play behind many of my childhood idols. When I was fifteen, my dream was to play with these stars. When I was twenty-three, I got to play with them in my hometown. It was a dream come true.

"Earth Angel" by The Penguins was practically a national anthem in Southern California. When we backed up The Penguins at The Bunny, I recognized a young man in the audience named Sid. When I was seventeen, Sid and his friend Tom had broken into my parents' house and stolen all my records and expensive Sir Guy shirts. I'd worked hard to buy those records and clothes by washing dishes and working as a delivery boy. I called the Whittier Police. When they arrived, an officer asked who had recently visited our home. My father gave him the name of Sid's friend, Tom. The police immediately had their suspect. Tom had a long rap sheet and was on parole from the California Youth Authority (teenage prison). The cops stopped Tom and Sid as they were driving in East Whittier and found my shirts and records in their car. They were arrested for burglary and sent back to reform school.

It made me nervous to see Sid in the audience. I thought he might still be harboring thoughts of revenge. In my teenage years, Sid was the toughest kid in Whittier. I watched him from the stage as The Penguins sang "Earth Angel," playing out all possible scenarios in my mind. After the set, I walked to his table and shook his hand. He was friendly and respectful, and I was kiss-ass and obsequious. Later in the evening a friend said, "Sid wonders why you think he's so special. He said he was just a jailbird, while *you're* the one who's special. You're a musician!" I guess I couldn't erase the memory of Sid being the most bad-ass kid in Whittier; the kid nobody could beat in a fight. I was afraid of Sid at The Plush Bunny in 1966, and if he's still alive, I'd be scared of him today. He was one bad dude.

Over the following weeks in Whittier, I got to play with some of the most famous artists of doo-wop and R&B. I felt like a "Homecoming King." The list of stars was amazing! Sonny Knight with his hit "Confidential," Bobby Day with "Rockin' Robin," and Jessie Hill with "Ooh Poo Pa Doo." The Isley Brothers tore up the stage with "Twist & Shout," and Johnny "Guitar" Watson sang "Lonely Nights." Ron Holden sang his hit "Love You So," The Shields sang "You Cheated," Robert & Johnny sang "(You're Mine and) We Belong Together," and

The Five Satins filled the dance floor with their timeless hit, "In the Still of the Night."

We never needed to rehearse with these artists because we already knew many of their songs. Most of the doo-wop songs were easy with standard "ice cream" changes, as we musicians call them. In simple terms, they usually involved chord progressions of *one, minor sixth, fourth, one* (C, A minor, F, C), or *one, minor sixth, minor second, one* (C, A minor, D minor, C).

I've always loved The Coasters' music, and when I was a kid, their songs were food for my soul. I'd do almost anything to buy their records: wash dishes, cut lawns, or beg my parents for an advance on my allowance. "Searchin' " was my favorite Coasters' song, but I also loved "Young Blood" and "Poison Ivy." In fact, one of the first R&B songs I learned on piano was their hit, "Riot in Cell Block #9." When we backed up The Coasters at The Plush Bunny, I was in sideman heaven. If my hometown friends (and former enemies) had any lingering doubts about me, they were gone forever when they saw me play with that famous group!

After playing The Galaxy, The Hollywood Palladium, The Hullabaloo, and The Plush Bunny, I began to develop a good reputation. There were more experienced organists playing in South Central L.A., but they were strictly into jazz and never played outside the black area of town. This left me with *almost* no competition in the rest of Southern California.

One evening at The Plush Bunny, a well-dressed man approached me. He introduced himself as a theatrical agent and said, "I have an organ player who plays better than you!" I was nonchalant and unimpressed by his challenge. I'd played against the best, including Jimmy McGriff, Richard "Groove" Holmes, and "Baby Face" Willette. Like a gunfighter in the Old West, I said, "Bring your organ player to the club anytime you want."

The following weekend, the agent returned to The Plush Bunny with Billy Preston. I'd never heard of him, even though he was a regular on the TV show, *Shindig*. To my surprise, Billy was a great gospel organist, a good singer, and an outstanding showman. That night at The Plush Bunny, he used a combination of organ playing, singing, and showmanship in an attempt to dethrone me as "Hammond King of L.A." I hadn't realized that Billy was so talented, so after his performance I played my lifesaving version of "Summertime."

According to audience response, Billy and I finished the contest in a neck and neck draw. In the near future, Preston and I would duel again.

One of my most significant moments at The Plush Bunny ironically involved the Whittier Police. For many years, I felt I owed a debt to Sergeant Bill Spencer. From when I was a twelve-year-old kid and joined Spencer's "Whittier Junior Police" to when Bill sponsored our Road Gamblers car club, he had befriended me and tried to help me through my teens. Spencer always believed in my music, much more than my own parents. I loved the old man, and phoned him at police headquarters to let him know I was playing at The Plush Bunny.

When Sergeant Spencer walked into the club, I invited him to take a seat at Anne's table. I could see him watching me play, a smile of pride on his gruff Irish face. During the break, I joined him and Anne at our table. I was happy that the old policeman could see I'd come a long way from the Whittier jail and made something special out of my life. He was proud of me in 1966, but if he'd seen me in 1967, his pride would have turned to sorrow. He would have seen my dilated eyes and known that I'd become an amphetamine and barbituate pill-head like Johnny Cash. He might have cried.

Chapter 15

Etta James, Billy Preston

While playing The Plush Bunny, our band was offered a gig at The California Club in Los Angeles. It was a high-class black establishment and a favorite nightspot for such luminaries as Sam Cooke and Joe Tex. Etta James was scheduled to play for two weeks and needed a band. We had tremendous respect for Etta and loved her records. Great songs by a great singer! We decided to take a break from the "Bunny" for the rare opportunity to play with this goddess of soul.

When I first met Etta in the hallway between our dressing rooms at The California Club, I was in for a surprise. Dressed only in a black corset, her legs were covered with black and blue bruises. I had no idea what they were, and only later learned they were caused by injecting heroin. Her battle with drugs was much worse than mine would become the following year, because I never touched a needle.

Etta was nice to our band, and we liked her as a person as well as a singer. She wasn't the least bit arrogant or snobbish, but when we played together something was missing. She was at a low ebb in her career and it was obvious that her heart wasn't into her work. She sang some of her hits like "I'd Rather Go Blind," "All I Could Do Was Cry," and "Something's Got a Hold on Me," but filled most of her shows with cover songs by other artists, like Jimmy Reed's "Baby What You Want Me to Do." I thought she was singing these songs because they were easy for both her and our band. I didn't realize she'd recorded these cover songs in 1963 on a live album entitled, *Etta Rocks The House*, recorded at the New Era Club in Nashville, Tennessee. It sold many copies and is still popular today.

Besides the Jimmy Reed song, Etta sang Ray Charles's "What'd I Say," a song that requires a Wurlitzer electric piano. I didn't have access to a Wurlitzer, and had to play the intro on organ, which didn't sound nearly as strong and catchy. I thought this might upset her, but she just gave me a little smile as if to say, "That's OK, I understand." She also sang "Every Day I Have The Blues" by B.B. King and "Ooh Poo Pa Doo" by Jessie Hill.

When our first set with Etta James came to a close, she put her hands on top of my Hammond, leaned close to my ear and said, "Baby, you're a cookin' motherfucker on that organ!" Then she smiled and left the stage. Man, did that stir my soul and touch my heart. She was the most famous artist I'd ever worked with, and she liked my music!

Etta's contract expired after two weeks, and the club owner asked our band to play for another week. With Bobby Angelle and Arthur Adams, we managed to attract decent crowds, but the management thought they needed a special guest artist for Saturday night. That guest artist was none other than Billy Preston.

When Billy challenged me at The Plush Bunny, I hadn't bothered to upstage him before he played. Consequently, the contest ended in a close draw. But I was on my home turf at The Plush Bunny, the audience made up of Chicanos and whites. At The California Club, I was on Billy Preston's turf, playing for a black audience. The crowd might lean in his favor. I decided to burn Billy before he had a chance to burn me. We had one song left to play before his performance, and I decided to play my rendition of "Summertime," a song I didn't think Billy could match. When I ended with powerful church-like "Amen" chords (Fm Cm7), the all-black audience honored me with a standing ovation.

While people were still on their feet, I grabbed the microphone and yelled, "Ladies and gentlemen, Mr. Billy Preston!"

I left the organ and took a seat with Anne and some friends. We were astonished to see what Billy Preston did when he reached the stage. He sat on my organ bench but never played a note! He sang a few songs with the band, but never touched the keys. Preston refused to compete with me after "Summertime." Several years later, Billy went to England and worked with The Beatles and The Rolling Stones. He also recorded two hit records of his own, "Will It Go Round in Circles" and "Nothing From Nothing." Billy toured with The Stones and played keyboards on The Beatles' mega-hit "Get Back." I might have received an ovation at The California Club, but Billy got the last hurrah.

Nine years later in 1975, I saw Billy again when I was playing at the Starwood in Hollywood with Delaney Bramlett. He entered our dressing room and said, "Hi, Rick," smiled with the now-familiar gap between his front teeth and shook my hand. He had reached a place in music I would never see, but still remembered who won our last organ battle. A few months later, I watched Billy playing my arrangement of "Summertime" on national TV.

After The California Club, Al and the Originals returned to The Plush Bunny. At the same time, Bobby Angelle got a regional hit on Money Records with "Love the Way You Love," and guitarist Arthur Adams signed a contract with Kent Records. Even our drummer Ron Ringo signed with a small record label. Ron left the band, and the group began to disintegrate. Within a few weeks, I was unemployed.

For the past two years, I'd been making about $1,000 per week in today's dollars with Al and the Originals, and in my youthful naïveté believed it would last forever. Suddenly, Anne, the kids, and I were faced with poverty. While I looked for work with other bands, the bank repossessed my beautiful white Cadillac. That was a real heartbreaker, as the car was symbolic of my long sought-after success in music. Our telephone was disconnected, electricity turned off, and our gas meter plugged shut. City water was turned off, and even our trash service discontinued. I had to bury our garbage in the back yard. On cold winter nights, we piled blankets over the kids while we slept beneath rugs and coats. For food, we ran a charge account with a Helms bread truck and filled up on donuts and bread. We hocked almost everything we owned, from my tape recorder to Anne's diamond wristwatch. We boiled spaghetti on a bar-b-que, using newspaper and pieces of wood for fuel. We couldn't pay the rent on our house and received a notice to quit.

I never wanted Anne to work, although she was highly qualified in the mortgage business. It was a matter of foolish pride, coupled with jealousy on my part. I was down and out, and afraid she might meet someone else. Such fears were not completely unfounded. My life was a mess, and I didn't deserve her. Drugs had destroyed most of the person she loved. But after we'd stagnated in poverty for months, Anne and I agreed there was no choice. She would seek employment.

Anne searched the want ads, and after a brief interview was hired by a mortgage company in L.A. as an escrow officer. The money she earned allowed us to pay rent on a small apartment and fix the Mustang. I hated every moment she worked, and hated myself even more. I took care of the kids during the day and searched for club work at night. I never gave up trying to find a job, but my reputation with pills had spread across the L.A. area.

Occasionally I was able to play gigs with Bobby Angelle and Arthur Adams, but they were only one-night stands and whatever money I earned was quickly spent. My grandparents sent us a few dollars from their Social Security checks, but nothing could replace a steady income. To make matters worse, Anne and I joined the ongoing fad of the mid-1960s and began taking "whites" (amphetamines) and "reds" (Seconal), easily available from drug pushers in most bars and nightclubs.

The "whites," popular with truck drivers and others who needed to stay awake for long hours, induced a feeling of euphoria, similar to cocaine. They provided two or three days of owl-eyed conversation, seemingly on the highest intellectual levels, in babbling efforts of solving the mysteries of the universe. The "whites," "bennies," "uppers," or whatever they were called, were dangerous because after several days without sleep, they induced extreme paranoia. But they didn't cause a person to become violent unless mixed with another (and opposite) drug, a barbiturate or "downer" like Seconal, which we called "red devils" in California.

This was a dangerous combination and caused Anne and me to spend weekends without sleep and indulge in terrible fights that still haunt me with guilt. During one altercation, based upon nothing but drug-induced insanity, the fight became violent and I slapped my dear Annie. I felt so guilty that I left the house with a revolver, intent upon suicide. I couldn't gain the courage to shoot myself so I returned to the house, found my Boy Scout hatchet, and attacked my piano. I smashed the front of the instrument into splinters. It was a means of attacking myself.

After another horrendous fight, I decided to seek help. I tried to drive to a California State Hospital (nuthouse) and commit myself for treatment. Anne was the best part of my life, and I didn't want to lose her. I knew that pills were causing all of our troubles, and wanted to stop before it was too late. On the way to the hospital, my car ran out of gas. I took an empty gas can from the trunk and cut off a length of hose from a neighbor's yard, intent upon siphoning fuel from parked cars. I was in a residential neighborhood, examining a 1965 or 1966 Oldsmobile when two vicious dogs rushed toward me, their teeth bared for the kill. I flung the gas can and hose into some bushes and climbed atop the Oldsmobile. Lights came on, and two men rushed from their house to find me standing on the roof of their car. I told them I was merely walking home when the dogs attacked. Fortunately, they believed my story and called off their knowledgeable beasts.

I climbed down from the car and walked back to my stalled vehicle. As I was pondering how to steal some gasoline, a police car slowly approached and pulled to the curb. The officer asked if I needed help, and I asked him to take me to a hospital. He shined a bright flashlight into my eyes and could see I was high on drugs. I remember him saying, "I've got the hospital for you." I was handcuffed and shoved into the police car.

When we reached the Pomona Police Station, I was taken to a small room and interrogated by a detective. He seemed to be a kind man and said, "I can understand people taking 'speed.' It makes them alert and keeps them awake. But I can't understand why people take 'downers.' They make people mean and crazy." The detective knew exactly what was wrong with me, but I wouldn't confess. I told him I was just drunk.

The detective turned me over to a jailer, who led me through some barred doors and down a long hallway. I expected to be placed into a conventional jail cell, but the jailer took me to a strange-looking steel door with a peephole in the middle. When he unlocked the door, I saw that the entire room was covered with soft material. The walls and ceiling looked like they were upholstered with canvas, and the floor was covered with thick, yellow rubber. There was a drain in the middle of the floor, designed for vomit and urine. I had never seen anything like it before. A padded cell. I told the jailer that I wasn't crazy and didn't belong in that room. He pulled out his nightstick and said, "Do you want me to help you get inside?" I entered the room, and the door locked behind me. I lay upon the rubber floor and thought about my life. I cried myself to sleep with thoughts of guilt and self-hatred.

Before I realized what was happening, I was awakened by a shoe in the middle of my back. The morning guard hadn't kicked me but merely "shoved" me into consciousness. Nightstick in hand, he led me back down the hallway. I thought I was going to be released, but instead was guided to another area of the jail and placed in a large cell occupied entirely by black men. There were six to eight bunk beds and a TV camera on the wall. The camera gave me some relief, and I hoped the cops were watching in case I was attacked or sodomized.

One of the black men approached me and said, "Hey, aren't you the organ player from the Jewell Room?" When I nodded yes, most of the men in the cell realized who I was. They became friendly and treated me like a "brother." One man asked, "What did they bust you for, alcohol?" I answered, "No, Seconal." The man laughed. Most of my jail-mates had been arrested for alcohol-related issues, like drunk driving or being drunk in public. I felt safe enough to lie down on my cot and rest.

After a few moments, I heard the loud rattling of jailhouse keys as our cell door opened. From my bunk, I smelled the wonderful aroma of food. I hadn't eaten in several days and my hunger was ferocious. We were served Swanson TV dinners on aluminum trays. I joined the other men at a table and scarfed down my meatloaf with a plastic spoon. When my jail-mates saw how hungry I was, they kindly shared their food with me. I ate so much that I became dizzy. I ran to a toilet and retched. My sick body expelled all the food, and I could taste the sickening residue of drugs. I had never reached a point so low and it should have taught me a lesson, but it taught me nothing. I continued to take pills for another year.

Within tragedy, there is usually some degree of humor. One such instance occurred when Anne tried to awaken me after several days without sleep. She shook me to no avail. In a final attempt, she poured ice water on my face. I awoke in a rage of insanity and took a cold electric blanket from our bed. I covered Anne with the blanket like an Indian papoose and used the cord from the blanket to tie her into a bundle. With Anne bound on the floor, I went back to sleep. Being a bold Scot, Anne quickly freed herself and poured more water on my face. When I tried to wrap her in the blanket again, she struck me on the hip with a Spinata wine bottle. I fell to the floor in agony. It was one fight that Anne managed to win. Hats off to Annie!

The Cadillac was gone, and Anne's Mustang wouldn't start without major repairs. One of our Whittier friends gave us a 1958 Ford with a bad radiator. He was high on pills and didn't mind giving away an old car. We had no money for gas, so once again I sneaked down a darkened street and tried to steal gasoline from a parked car. I took a piece of hose and inserted it into a neighbor's gas tank. I placed the other end of the hose in my mouth and sucked. A huge blast of gasoline flooded my mouth and throat, and I fell to the ground. I couldn't catch my breath. I hid beneath a bush as a car passed with blazing headlights and prepared to die from suffocation. Slowly, gasp by gasp, I regained the ability to breathe and staggered home.

On another occasion, Bobby Angelle was booked to play "The Soul-Time Review" at the Hollywood Palladium, a concert produced by a local radio station, and I was to accompany him on organ. For some odd reason, Eartha Kitt was also on the bill. I remembered my parents watching her on the *Ed Sullivan Show*. They might have liked her music, but as a teenager I found her singing and pseudo-French accent obnoxious and silly. Our show at the Palladium featured black R&B singers who sang the music of the day, not songs from the distant past. Why Eartha Kitt was booked with a soul singer like Bobby Angelle, I'll never know.

After we finished our set, I needed to use the restroom that was located in Eartha's large dressing room. Even though we were performing on the same show, Eartha and her manager refused to let me use the toilet. They were rude and downright mean. I left the artists' area and watched Eartha onstage while I stood in line to use the public restroom. From where I was standing, I could see people leaving the theater. They'd bought tickets to hear Angelle and other R&B singers, not Eartha Kitt with her kittenish "Santa Baby" song. I took pleasure in the fact that people didn't like her music. She was an arrogant bitch and deserved to be snubbed. In fact, if she'd been playing in a less civilized area, she might have needed chicken wire for protection from flying beer bottles!

When Anne and I left the Palladium, we couldn't locate our car. We searched Sunset Boulevard and Hollywood Boulevard, but couldn't find the 1958 Ford. Bobby Angelle had to drive us home in his '65 Chevy. Two weeks later, I suddenly remembered where we'd parked the car. Anne and I took a bus to Hollywood and found the old Ford, patiently waiting for us on a side street.

In another speed-freak episode, I decided that my Hammond organ was too heavy. It weighed over 400 pounds, and I didn't have an organ dolly. My band mates and I had to carry the big, bulky organ in and out of every club we played. I got some tools from the garage and took the organ completely apart. I removed both keyboards, the tone generator and most of the wires. In a coffee can, I placed every screw, washer and fitting that I deemed expendable and threw them into the trash. After I reassembled the Hammond, it remained just as heavy.

Looking for work after the demise of Al and the Originals, Anne and I drove to every nightclub we could find in the L.A. area, hoping to find a band with a B3 on stage. When we found such a club, I'd ask to sit in on organ. In every instance, I outplayed the band's organist, but I had a problem: I was an arrogant bastard, high on pills. As a result, I was never offered a decent gig. I was a pill-head and a cocky bastard.

Eventually, I would find a job with people who were even more drug-involved, although it took me some time to realize this. All that mattered was that I'd be playing with a group that was signed to one of the best record companies in Hollywood and put on a retainer of about $500 per week in today's dollars. It was another chance of a lifetime.

Chapter 16
A&M Records, Hollywood

A&M Records was located at the old Charlie Chaplin Studios in Hollywood. In an ironic twist of fate, it was the same studio where my father performed as an extra in Chaplin's classic movie, *City Lights*, in 1931. Every time I drove through the security gates and presented my ID to the guards, I thought of my father. I could see him as a young man, walking through the same entrance. While I doubt he would have been proud of me, it might have been a bit of payback for his criticism.

The year was 1968 and A&M was just beginning to record artists other than co-owner Herb Alpert and his Tijuana Brass. I was hired to play on a debut album by Joanne Vent, a pretty blonde with a powerful voice. She might have emerged as one of America's top female vocalists had it not been for drugs, alcohol, and a poor choice of material. Rather than filling her album with new and original songs, Joanne and her producers decided to take the dangerous path of covering hits by other artists. Songs by Blood, Sweat and Tears, Bobby "Blue" Bland, and James Brown dominated the effort.

We were scheduled to rehearse at A&M Studios five days per week. The engine of Anne's Mustang had been repaired, although the entire trunk section was smashed and buckled from a rear-end collision. On my first drive to rehearsal, while listening to the car radio and not paying close attention to my driving, I hit the bumper of an old pickup truck on a freeway on-ramp. The accident didn't damage the truck, but ruined the front of the Mustang. I had to use a rope to tie down the hood, and arrived at A&M Studios in this rolling wreck of an automobile. I stopped at the iron gate, showed my ID, and was allowed to enter the employees' parking area.

Our rehearsal area was in a large building from the era of silent films, probably the same room where my father had worked as an actor. It took four men to carry my organ inside to a large platform. On the same platform was Lee Michaels' Hammond B3, connected to six Leslie speaker cabinets. I could only imagine what power I could generate if I could play his B3, but I didn't want to mess around with Lee's settings. Although I never met him, I respected Michaels. I considered myself to be a better musician, but he was a star and I was just a sideman. Lee could sing and had an infectious and original rock-organ style. He'd have never survived the black nightclubs I'd played, but he was great with white audiences. Other artists at A&M admired our group. Joanne could out-sing most of them and our band could outplay them. Energized by amphetamines, we played hard and strong. A&M owners Herb Alpert and Jerry Moss loved our music. We had talent, but it takes more than talent to cut hit records.

A&M Records booked us at a local nightclub as a means of exposure in Hollywood. Opening the show for us was a new band featuring three male singers called Three Dog Night, soon to become one of the most successful groups of the late 1960s and early '70s. We had no fear of this new group and thought it odd that they had three lead singers. We sat in our dressing room ignoring their set as our sax player Michael McCormack offered me a small packet of white powder. He told me the packet contained methamphetamine, and I should snort it up my nose. I was afraid to snort the meth because it made me think of heroin, a drug I'd never touched and never would. I didn't want to look like a coward, so I took the small packet, poured it into a glass of water and drank it down.

After Three Dog Night finished their set, our band hit the stage with great confidence. "Three Dog" was good but lacked the bluesy musicianship of our band and the soulful power of Joanne's voice. As soon as she began to sing, the audience belonged to her and our band. Executives from A&M Records who'd come to hear us were happy and said we'd played a great show. Stoned or not, our first gig was a success.

After the show, Anne and I were driving home on the Hollywood Freeway when we saw a brilliant shower of sparks on the pavement just ahead of us. To our amazement, we watched as an upside-down Volkswagen skidded down the road on its back. The car must have blown a front tire and flipped, coming to a halt in the fast lane of the Interstate. I parked our Mustang on the right shoulder of the freeway and ran to the car. The passengers were in imminent danger of being killed. An oncoming driver might fail to notice their inverted VW and crash into it. I opened the door and found three women piled upon each other. I pulled them from the car as quickly as I could and guided them to a roadside callbox where they could phone for help. Anne and I drove the rest of the way home, knowing that we'd helped save three women's lives.

About two weeks later, it was time to cut Joanne's album, titled *The Black and White of it is The Blues*. I drove the wrecked Mustang to the recording studio, fortified by a few "whites" and maybe even a "red." I walked into the room like a star. After all, I was supposed to be one of the best organists in California. Alas, I was in for a terrible surprise. Other than our band, the studio was filled with sober, professional studio musicians. There was a large horn section, string section and other serious musicians. I'd thought that people were supposed to get high when they recorded, but this session was no place for pill-heads with frazzled brains. I became nervous and paranoid.

The producer, Larry Marks, seemed to know more about playing keyboards than I did, at least when it came to playing chords. I was embarrassed when he left the control booth and tried to show me how to play my charts. Larry said I was playing my chord inversions all wrong. I couldn't read music, and depended upon reading the chord symbols and playing them the way I wanted, Larry Marks wanted specific voicings for effect, placing different notes on top, playing some notes of the chords close together and others spread out, or leaving some chord tones out altogether. I knew virtually nothing about voicing. I was loaded on pills and couldn't concentrate. It would take this session to make me realize that being a studio musician is much more difficult than playing on stage. It takes concentration and a sharp mind, not a drug induced semi-coma. When Joanne's album was released to the public, I could barely hear my organ in the background. Maybe I'd earned some good karma from helping the women on the freeway because within the same year I'd be given another chance to record with a major label.

GOOD DEED results in sale for Ricky Sutherland, an enterprising Whittier Scout. He turned down money for his good deed.

Refuses Money For Good Deed

"A Good Deed Everyday" is the slogan of all Boy Scouts and, as Mrs. G. McKenzie of Whittier will attest, a local 11-year-old Scout typified the Scout and the slogan one day recently.

Young Ricky Sutherland of Boy Scout Troop 80, who lives at 637 Maulsby Dr., was canvassing the neighborhood recently selling tickets to the Scout Circus to be staged in Los Angeles in June.

When he rang the door bell at the McKenzie home, 607 Russell St., he heard moans from within and a call for help. He entered the home to find Mrs. McKenzie on the floor, where she had fallen after injuring her ankle.

Called Husband

The slender youth helped the woman to a chair, fetched a glass of water, and then called her husband at his place of employment, telling him the circumstances.

Young Sutherland remained with the injured woman until her husband arrived, and then aided in caring for her until she was comfortable.

When McKenzie offered him money for his help, the boy refused, saying it was his good deed for the day. The youth's father, John K. Sutherland, is a Scout committeeman.

After Mrs. McKenzie was comfortable, Ricky prepared to leave, but not before completing his mission.

He sold the McKenzies two tickets to the Scout Circus.

Earliest photo of Rick at piano,
although he started playing at age 9.
From Rick Allen's private collection.

Rick's car club, Whittier, 1959.
From Rick Allen's private collection.

(Left) Hometown hero, age 11, Whittier, CA.
From Rick Allen's private collection.

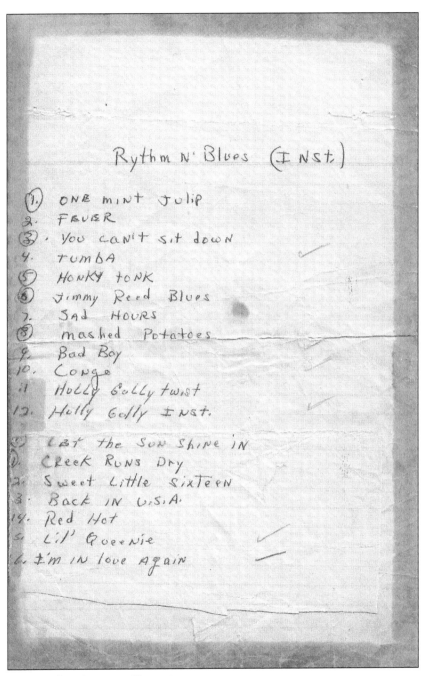

First song list, The Bonnevilles, 1961.
From Rick Allen's private collection.

Telethon, Marquette, MI, 1961. Left to right: John ?, Larry Lynne, Paul Edwards, Rick Allen.
From Rick Allen's private collection.

711 Club, Columbus, Ohio.
From Rick Allen's private collection.

**The Bonnevilles, 1962. Left to right: Paul Edwards, Tom Hahn, Rick Allen,
Larry Lynne (in front).**
From Rick Allen's private collection.

'Skunks' Will Dress the Part, Too

If, after seeing the Beatles, you were one of those who asked, "What next?", here are the Skunks with the answer. The Milwaukee rock 'n' roll group was known as the Bonnevilles before the Beatles demonstrated the importance of a gimmick. Left to right are: Larry Lynne, 1923 S. 10th st.; Rick Allen, 2706 W. Bobolink av.; Duane Lunde, 6603 W. Beloit rd., West Allis, Tony Klop, 1426 E. Howard av. The f[...] have dyed their hair black with wh[...] stripes down the sides. "Two beautici[...] worked on us for two days," Allen s[...] They appear at Monreal's, 1566 W. [...] tional av. They plan to get "skunk sui[...] to match their hair. —Journal P[...]

The Skunks, Milwaukee, 1964.
From Rick Allen's private collection.

(Left) Tom Fabré with Saxophone.
Courtesy of Jean Kennerson.

Rick jamming in Watts, 1966.
From Rick Allen's private collection.

Bobby Angelle.
From Rick Allen's private collection.

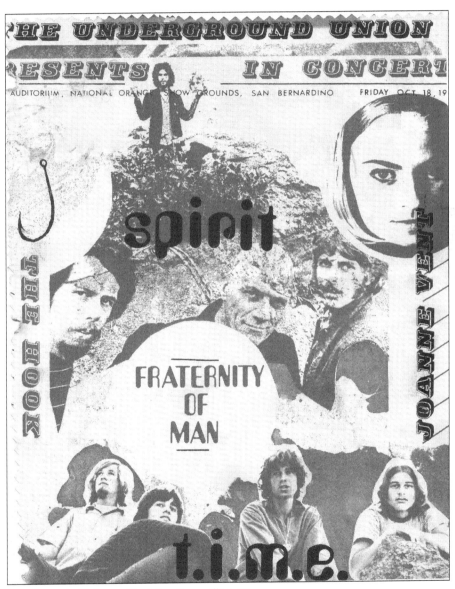

Concert with Joanne Vent, San Bernardino, CA.
From Rick Allen's private collection.

The Hullabaloo, Hollywood, CA.
From Rick Allen's private collection.

Blue Rose Band, 1969. Left to right: (top) Dave Thomson, Rick Allen, Chuck Morgan, Terry Furlong, (bottom) Dave, Rick, Chuck, Terry.
From Rick Allen's private collection.

(left) Rick and Delaney at Rock 'n' Roll Ranch.
From Rick Allen's private collection.

Rick and Delaney Bramlett.
From Rick Allen's private collection.

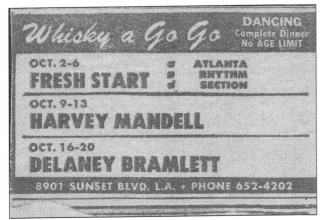

Delaney at Whisky a Go Go, Hollywood.
Courtesy of Joey D. Vieira.

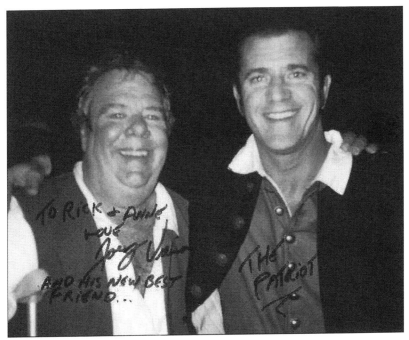

Rick's Manager, Joey D. Vieira, and Mel Gibson.
Courtesy of Joey D. Vieira.

(left) Rick at Madison Square Garden, New York.
From Rick Allen's private collection.

Bonnie Bramlett at Elvis' Graceland, Memphis.
From Rick Allen's private collection.

Big Johnny Thomassie, drummer, with Bonnie's tour bus.
From Rick Allen's private collection.

Robert Wilson with Bonnie's bus.
From Rick Allen's private collection.

Some of Rick's recordings.
From Rick Allen's private collection.

Ernie "Mother-in-Law" K-Doe.
Courtesy of Vernon Dugas.

Ernie K-Doe at Storyville, New Orleans.
From Rick Allen's private collection.

Rick with Allen Toussaint at Sea Saint Studios, New Orleans.
From Rick Allen's private collection.

Rick Allen playing Hammond B3, New Orleans.
From Rick Allen's private collection.

Studio shot with Freddy Fender, New Orleans. Left to right: assistant engineer, Robert Wilson, Dickie Taylor, Rick, assistant engineer, Roger Branch, Freddy Fender.
From Rick Allen's private collection.

Studio shot, Freddy Fender, Rick, Dicky Taylor.
From Rick Allen's private collection.

Studio shot, Robert "Barefootin" Parker and Rick.
From Rick Allen's private collection.

Rick and Anne's 25th Anniversary.
From Rick Allen's private collection.

presents this certificate to

Rick Allen

For Your Participation as a

Musician

on the GRAMMY®Award-Nominated Album

"Gloryland"
(The Dukes of Dixieland)

In the Category of

Best Pop/Contemporary Gospel Album

42nd GRAMMY® Awards Year 1999

Rick's Grammy Nomination.
From Rick Allen's private collection.

Rick's Session Work

From Rick Allen's private collection.

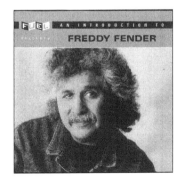

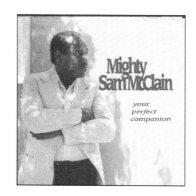

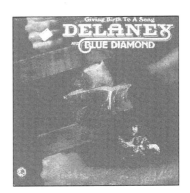

Dear Rick & Anne,

May you draw strength

in this difficult time

from those who care for you

and hold you

close in heart.

Otis Rush

06

Card from Otis Rush and his wife, after Katrina
From Rick Allen's private collection.

Chapter 17
Dr. John, Bobby Angelle

"I don't like these mountain roads; they get my nerves jumpin'," Bobby said as he blessed himself with the sign of the cross. It was the summer of 1968 and I was driving soul singer Bobby Angelle to his producer's home in Laurel Canyon in the Hollywood Hills. "These aren't mountains," I replied. "They're just little hills." But to Angelle, my words meant nothing. He was from flat Louisiana, and any hill over twenty feet high was a mountain to him.

Angelle's song "I Love the Way You Love" was #6 on L.A.'s R&B charts and had caught the ear of Liberty Records producer Steve LaVere. His plan was to break into the national R&B market. I liked LaVere's house. It was large but unpretentious and filled with relics of the early 1950s. I remember seeing a five-cent Coke machine, a jukebox, and even an old Texaco gas pump. I felt comfortable in these Bohemian surroundings. After we played a tape of Angelle's new songs, LaVere called Liberty Records and booked our first session with Mac Rebennack (Dr. John) as our arranger. "I've heard of Mac," Angelle said. "He's a good musician, him!"

The following week we drove to Dr. John's apartment in Hollywood to rehearse. He and Angelle were both from Louisiana but sounded *much* different. Dr. John's baritone was nasal, and sounded like a cross between Louis Armstrong and a Bourbon Street barker. Angelle's tenor often flipped into falsetto, his accent a combination of Louisiana Cajun-French and Southern black.

I accompanied Angelle on piano as he sang his songs for Mac. When we finished, Dr. John growled, "I'll arrange *tree* of deese songs. I don't like the ress of 'em!" Angelle looked at Dr. John in astonishment. "Let me get this straight. You only arrange songs you *like*?" "Yeah," cracked Dr. John, "I only arrange songs I like!" Angelle said, "You supposed to be an arranger, yes? They payin' you to arrange songs? And you, (going into falsetto) *only arrange songs you like?* Where you from, you?"

"I'm N'awlins Creole," growled Dr. John. "I'm Creole too," replied Angelle, "I'm from Lafayette, me. You must be crazy, you!" And so it went, on into the afternoon. All I could do was laugh and be happy that a song I wrote was among the *"tree"* that Dr. John liked. Driving home, Angelle kept saying, "That crazy jackass. He's no real arranger, him. He's a crazy jackass!"

Our session was scheduled at Gold Star Studios in Hollywood, and I was determined not to make the same mistakes I'd made at A&M Records with Joanne Vent. I carefully memorized the songs we were scheduled to record and studied up on reading chord charts with symbols like D/S (*dal segno*, meaning from the sign, the "sign" usually being an S dissected by a diagonal line with a dot on either side), D/C (*da capo*, meaning from the "top"), D/S *al fine* (from the sign to the ending), and more. Pretty complicated shit for me as a self-taught musician, but a worthwhile study. Ironically, I wouldn't need any of this newly acquired knowledge for our session.

When Angelle and I arrived at the studio, Dr. John was nowhere to be found. Eventually, he strolled in with his musicians: a piano player, a conga player, a bassist, and a drummer whose cymbals were draped with heavy chains. Dr. John came with a handful of blank chord charts! He hadn't written arrangements for our songs and proceeded to scratch them out on studio time. Not really arrangements at all, but just basic chord changes that didn't involve any of my tedious homework. When the session began, Mac played guitar while sitting on a stool as if directing the band. I was assigned to a Hammond B3.

Over a period of several hours, we managed to cut the rhythm tracks for the songs Mac said he liked. The tracks were nice, although the congas and chains altered the feel and took the music in a different direction from what Angelle and I intended. The tracks were clean, my playing was never criticized and I knew the songs could be improved with overdubs. While listening to a playback, I suggested to producer LaVere that we add female background singers. He agreed, and scheduled a vocal session.

The following week, Angelle recorded his lead vocals, and the girl singers arrived at Gold Star Studios. I was happy to see that our producer had hired Clydie King, Shirley Matthews, and Venetta Fields, the best background vocalists in Los Angeles. These women had recorded with many artists including Ike and Tina Turner and Ray Charles, but they were uncertain about what we wanted them to sing on Angelle's songs. Their uncertainty lit my creative fuse, and I rushed to their aid.

During my three years as a speed freak, there were times when amphetamines helped open doors of creativity in my mind. Being familiar with soul and gospel music, I instructed the girls exactly which notes to sing. I asked them to sing chords that were church-like, with phrases ending on dominant seventh harmonies. The singers liked me and were surprised that a white boy could think so "black." I stood in front of the singers and directed them like an orchestra conductor. When all was finished, our producer was pleased and wrote me a check for about $700 in today's currency, just for helping the girls. When the record was released, the label included my name as vocal arranger.

Unfortunately, Angelle wanted both sides of the 45 to consist of his compositions, saving my song for his next single. We'd only recorded three songs, and in order to release my song, titled "I Still Need You," we'd need another session to record the "B" side. Liberty was watching the market's reaction to Angelle's first single, and if it didn't sell, the game would end. False modesty aside, my song was much more commercial than Angelle's. It employed interesting Motown-style chord changes, a "catchy hook" chorus and a memorable horn-section riff. It was in the category of records that were selling in the rhythm and blues market. Even Bobby's sister cried when she heard my song, and said it was beautiful. In contrast, Angelle's songs were weak and simplistic. As a result, the record was a failure and Angelle's career came to a slow and painful end.

The greatest male singer I'd ever known died in obscurity at the early age of fifty-two. When Anne and I learned of Bobby's death, we put his picture on my piano and played some of his records. Our silent tears searched until they found permanent residence in our hearts.

Chapter 18

Blue Rose Band

Linda Ronstadt, Albert King,
Delaney And Bonnie, Steve Allen

After my dreams of success with Bobby Angelle and Liberty Records faded, I got a call from Joey Vieira. He wanted to create a recording group with some of the best musicians in Los Angeles. I met with Joey at his beachfront home in Malibu, along with several other musicians, including guitarist Eddie Armen, singer Bobby Dee, drummer Tony DeZago, trumpet player Bobby Loya, and bassist Richard "Bird" Burdick.

In 1969, Joey Vieira and three partners founded Sound City Recording Studios, later to become one of the most important studios in L.A., recording superstars like Neil Young and Fleetwood Mac. Joey wanted to call our band "Nth," as in "the Nth degree," a catchy name but probably ahead of its time. We would have unlimited recording time at Sound City, free of charge. It could have been another chance of a lifetime, but our fate was doomed from the onset. Doomed because most of us were still taking "uppers" and "downers." We were functionally insane. We could play music, but we couldn't make plans, handle business affairs, or even *think*.

To make matters worse, our lead singer Bobby Dee had a hidden fear of the recording industry and was only comfortable singing top-40 hits by other artists in local nightclubs.

While we were trying to decide which songs to record, Joey kept us working by booking our band at various clubs around Los Angeles, including a bar in North Hollywood called The Little Hobbit. This club featured amateur topless dancers on weekends. Girls from age eighteen were allowed to strip topless on stage, and it was impossible not to stare at them. In my case, it was a matter of "You can look, but you better not touch!"

Most of the girls were pretty, but one was horribly ugly, with stringy black hair and a nose like a beak. I'll call her "Pelican Nose." She must have noticed me snickering behind her back because she sought revenge. Driving home after the gig, I noticed an old car following me, driven by Pelican Nose. She followed me down the Golden State Freeway and onto the San Bernardino Freeway, driving near my rear bumper and then passing me. When her car got in front of mine, she would apply her brakes, red taillights blaring. I had to jam on my brakes to avoid crashing into her. After she grew weary of this game, she tried to run me off the road. Her car edged toward my driver's side and forced me onto the shoulder. Pelican Nose was trying to kill me!

Still driving on the shoulder, I floored my car into passing gear. After Anne had returned to work, we managed to buy a 1965 Cadillac de Ville. It was four years old, but it was fast! The Cadillac quickly gained momentum and passed Pelican Nose. I swerved from the shoulder and cut in front of her car. The Caddy decided to show its power and climbed to over one hundred miles per hour, leaving Pelican Nose in its exhaust. I could see her headlights growing smaller in my rear view mirror as I raced home to El Monte.

Before going to our apartment, I stopped by the police station and told the desk sergeant that someone had tried to kill me on the freeway. He looked at me with complete disinterest, sipped his coffee, took a bite of a donut, and said, "The freeway is out of our jurisdiction. You'll have to talk to the Highway Patrol." By this time, Pelican Nose was miles away. I had no choice but to give up and drive home. Fortunately, I would never see Miss Pelican again.

Our band never performed as Nth, the name being saved for our first album. One night at our apartment while Anne and the kids were sleeping, I was wide awake from speed. While lying on the living room carpet with pencil and paper, I composed an original song for our band. I managed to write this song without a piano or any other instrument, every part including horn section riffs entirely in my head. Our lead singer, Bobby Dee, had a voice somewhat like David Clayton-Thomas of Blood, Sweat and Tears, so I wrote the song with that style in mind. The song, titled "You Came into My Life," was inspired by my love for Anne. Along with the lyrics, I came up with original and interesting chord changes. I scrawled a five line stave, wrote out the chord changes, and even the lead notes for our trumpet player.

Since our band had only one horn player, I figured out how to make one trumpet sound like a trumpet section. I decided this could be accomplished by stacking Bobby Loya's horn parts on four separate tracks by means of overdubbing and then mixing the tracks together. Track #1 would be the lead line, the second and third tracks the third and fifth harmonies, and the fourth track a repeat of the lead line but played an octave higher. It was the only song we recorded at Sound City with Nth, and believe it or not, my ideas worked. But our project went no further than that song. Other band members couldn't write music, and I was in no condition to compose an entire album while playing clubs six nights per week. More importantly, our lead singer started to cause trouble in the band.

All the musicians in Nth were high-caliber players, but our lead singer Bobby Dee, an acne-faced Chicano, was never ready for a recording career. He was content to spend his life playing clubs and wanted to copy Top 40 songs off the jukebox. In order to rid the band of musicians with higher expectations, he began treating us with disrespect, as if he were King Shit and we were his toilet. Our bass player and drummer both quit the band and were replaced by mediocre club musicians. I didn't quit because Anne and I needed the money. When Bobby Dee realized this, he told Anne that I was chasing other women at the clubs we played. This was an absolute lie, but it caused Anne and me to have a terrible fight, fueled by pills and madness. The neighbors called the police, and we were almost evicted from our apartment.

After the cops had left, I stood in our parking lot and looked up at the starry sky. I didn't believe in God, but I made a promise to the universe. In the summer of 1969, I vowed to never take Seconal again. I've kept my promise for over forty years, and the mere thought of those pills turns my stomach.

Over the ensuing years, there were times when Anne and I had marital spats like most couples, but never another violent fight.

I told Joey Vieira that I couldn't work with Bobby Dee any longer, and asked him what he considered to be the best new band in Los Angeles. After a few moments of thought, he answered, "Blue Rose." Acting on Joey's advice, Anne and I went to hear them at the Brass Ring nightclub in Encino. Simply put, they were great! They played a combination of blues, R&B, and hardcore rock along with vocal ballads with perfect harmonies like Crosby, Stills, and Nash.

Blue Rose was led by a charismatic, multi-talented guitarist and singer named Terry Furlong. Terry could play blues guitar and incorporate it into rock songs in new and original ways. He was also an exceptionally good singer, both alone and as part of the three-part harmonies at which Blue Rose excelled. The rest of the band consisted of Chuck Morgan, a powerhouse "in-the-pocket" drummer and Dave Thomson, an inventive and talented bass player. The band's only weakness was their keyboard player, who played without feeling and added nothing to the group. I felt my style of playing would complement Blue Rose and sat in at the Brass Ring, easily burning their organist. After the set, Dave Thomson said, "You've got to be our organ player!" I was about to enter the world of "hippie rock." I began playing with Blue Rose six nights per week, often trading sets with a new group called Delaney and Bonnie.

I let my hair grow long and began to learn this new style of music. There were moments during songs that were unfamiliar to me, segments where the band stayed on the same chord for long periods and the soloists tripped out with improvisation. This was nothing like the structured rhythm and blues music I was accustomed to, but it was interesting and fun. When my turn came to trip out, I learned to incorporate all sorts of styles in my playing. I played riffs that sounded like Bach, then went to blues and rhythmic glissandos. Unfortunately, there are no recordings of my playing with Blue Rose other than a distorted tape from one of our concerts.

By this time, I'd listened to Jimi Hendrix and tried to emulate his style on the B3. I felt as if I were somehow faking the whole thing by trying to sound "psychedelic." I didn't learn until later that Jimi himself was a blues musician, just tripping-out with his fantastic chops and sound effects. I was still a blues boy trying to fit in with the crowd of flower children, with their lifestyle of free love and psychedelic drugs. I was afraid to try LSD, and never felt conversationally at ease with members of Blue Rose. They were "experienced" while I was naïve about oriental philosophy and other lessons learned from psychedelic adventures.

Blue Rose was booked as opening act for Linda Ronstadt at California Polytechnic College in Pomona. This was an important event for me because it would be the first time my grandparents would see me perform. I was twenty-six and had played in various bands for almost eight years, seesawing between success and poverty. My grandfather was helping with payments on my Hammond organ and often tried to convince me to get a regular job. It only took him seeing (and hearing) me on stage for one concert to change his mind forever.

Anne drove my grandparents from their home in Santa Ana to the Pomona concert. From the stage, I could see them sitting in the auditorium bleachers. Blue Rose opened the show, and when my turn came to sing, I dedicated a song I wrote called "Always Be Your Friend" to my grandfather, who was about to celebrate his ninetieth birthday. When I sang the song, I cried. My voice broke as tears streamed down my face. My parents never liked my music, but my grandparents had always been amazed at my ability. "Let's have some music, Ricky," my grandmother would often say, and I'd take a seat at the piano. My grandparents had watched me trying to learn music since I was seven years old, but had never seen me play professionally. Now was my chance to show them what I could do on stage. When my song ended, there was considerable applause and Grandpa never asked me to get a regular job again.

When a review of the concert was published in a local paper, we were excited to read the headline, "Blue Rose Pulls Surprise at Cal-Poly Concert." It said that Blue Rose "took the show" from Linda Ronstadt and that the best songs featured my organ. The promoter of the Pomona concert was a man named Gene Simmons, who took an immediate interest in our band. He was a master salesman, from selling new cars to promoting rock concerts. He had a knack for making money, and owned an expensive home on famous Mulholland Drive in the Hollywood Hills. When he offered to be our manager, we accepted and signed management contracts in the living room of the hippie shack where Terry, Dave, and Chuck were living in Van Nuys.

Simmons proceeded to book our band at many rock concerts in Southern California, opening for Frank Zappa, Spirit, Paul Butterfield, Michael Bloomfield, Jackie DeShannon, Boz Skaggs, and others. Invariably, our reviews were very positive. I enjoyed playing big concerts and felt at home with large audiences. Without a whisper of stage fright, I felt my destiny was being fulfilled.

Before opening the show for Jackie DeShannon at the Hollywood Palladium, I noticed the name of our band was misprinted on the list of performers. Instead of Blue Rose, the list read "Blue Roses." The master of ceremonies was the great Steve Allen, a man I'd always admired for his musicianship and wit. I approached him backstage and had the audacity to address him by his given name. "Steve," I said, "the list of band names is incorrect. Our band is called Blue Rose, not Blue Roses." Steve Allen smiled and told me not to worry. Taking a pen from his coat pocket, he corrected the error.

Blue Rose continued to play at the Brass Ring on a regular basis between concerts at local colleges and auditoriums. Blues legend Albert King thought he might sell more records with a white backup band, and came to the club to hear us. I introduced myself to Albert, told him I'd recorded with Sonny Boy Williamson in Chicago, and invited him to sit with Anne at our table. After listening to us play a few songs, Mr. King came on stage and jammed with us for almost an entire set. He wanted Blue Rose to be his band, but we weren't interested. We thought we were on the road to stardom, and didn't want to change direction, but instead Blue Rose was destined for self-destruction.

While Anne, the kids, and I were living in our own apartment in El Monte, the other members of Blue Rose were crammed together in a small one-bedroom hovel in Van Nuys. Living in such close proximity caused them to get on each other's nerves, leading bass player Dave and drummer Chuck to form an unjustified vendetta against lead singer/guitarist Terry Furlong. The anger between Dave, Chuck, and Terry grew more menacing each day, but I tried to remain neutral. When Blue Rose played a club owned by my friend Joey Vieira in Santa Monica called Joey's Head Quarters, the "simmering war" became entrenched rebellion.

On a Saturday night in front of a packed nightclub, Chuck Morgan stopped playing drums in the middle of a song while Terry was singing.

People were still dancing when Chuck brought the song to a sudden halt and kicked his drums off the stage, the cymbals crashing to the floor. Bass player Dave Thomson followed suit by turning off his amplifier and leaning his instrument against a wall. Then Chuck and Dave walked off the stage! The audience was rendered speechless as they watched this insanity. It was the most unprofessional act by musicians I'd ever seen, and especially embarrassing because the club owner was my friend.

Blue Rose was a special band. It had the potential of becoming very successful in the recording industry. Our rock version of the Temptations' "Losing You" was so strong and powerful that it could easily have been a hit record, just as Vanilla Fudge's rock version of the Supremes' "You Keep Me Hangin' On" topped the charts. Major labels were interested in signing us, but all was lost on that pitiful night in Santa Monica. Blue Rose died of self-inflicted wounds. Terry Furlong cut a faux Blue Rose album in the early 1970s with other musicians, and although the record was good, the magic of our original Blue Rose Band was gone. Terry later gained his much-deserved recognition by joining The Grass Roots and recording several hit records as their lead guitarist. After all my years in music, I've never known a finer musician than Terry Furlong.

I spent the next year recording for an independent production company at Devonshire Studios in North Hollywood, although my efforts at being a singer and songwriter proved to be in vain. My songs weren't Top 40, a category I loathed, but rather songs I considered to be creative with philosophical lyrics. But the opportunity to register hundreds of hours of studio experience and to work with musical genius Michael Omartian, who arranged and produced artists such as Rod Stewart and Billy Joel, was invaluable.

With Omartian, I had the opportunity to help write an arrangement for the L.A. Philharmonic's string section on a song I wrote called "Listen to the Leaders," an anti-war protest song during the Vietnam era. I played the notes on piano that I wanted the strings to play, and Michael wrote the charts. When the session was over, the first-chair violinist came into the control room and listened to a playback. When he heard the climatic ending, which involved an almost ethereal series of chord changes culminating in a strong crescendo, he said, "That's so emotional, I could scrub my wife's pantyhose on my goosebumps!"

Despite this, my producers couldn't find a record company that was interested in my songs. "Just not commercial enough" was the constant refrain. On the other hand, fate was about to take me on the most exciting yet frustrating journey of my musical life.

Chapter 19

Rock Star Tour, 1973

Rod Stewart, Ashford And Simpson,
Dave Mason, Steve Miller, Rory Gallagher,
Genya Ravan, Graham Nash

Shortly after my dreaded thirtieth birthday in March of 1973, I received a call from Eddie Tuduri, an excellent drummer who had worked with The Beach Boys, Jim Messina, and Rick Nelson. Eddie had been hired by The Rolling Stones' producer Jimmy Miller to complete an album by singer Genya Ravan for ABC Dunhill Records.

Genya's album was almost finished, but she wasn't happy with the project. The missing ingredient was straight-ahead rock 'n' roll. She wanted to record two new songs, "Keep On Growin' " and "Southern Celebration." Eddie Tuduri proceeded to hire Jerry McGee (guitarist for Barbra Streisand, Kris Kristofferson, Delaney and Bonnie), Rick Vito (future guitarist for Fleetwood Mac), studio bassist Bill Lincoln, and me to cut the new songs. Working with The Rolling Stones' producer was no small step for any musician. The Stones' recording engineer Andy Johns, along with the Stones trumpet player Jim Price completed the picture. When I arrived at the studio in Hollywood, I wanted to make a good impression. My desire to please Jimmy Miller would result in a bloodstained piano.

As an organ player, my fingers ("chops") weren't prepared for piano. Organ keys are much lighter to the touch, and my hands lacked the necessary calluses for piano. I took my place at a nine-foot Steinway grand. When the tape began to roll, I attacked the keys with the forcefulness of Little Richard. By the time the producer said, "Take three," my fingers were blistered, and when he said, "Take four," the blisters popped and became open wounds. I was in pain, but tried to ignore the agony. It might be my chance to play with the Stones! When we finished the rhythm tracks, the piano keys were streaked with blood.

Compared to the other material on Genya's album, "Keep on Growin' " and "Southern Celebration" were a welcomed relief. They were solid rock and "in the groove," with Genya's powerful vocals and Jerry McGee's slide guitar. My piano solo wasn't too shabby either. Unfortunately, it took another "bird" to fly "Keep on Growin' " to the top of the charts. In 1995, it would become a hit for Sheryl Crow. She must have heard our ABC session, because Sheryl's version was too close to be coincidental. In fact, when I first heard her version, I thought it was our record. "Oh man," I thought, "here comes my first gold record!" Alas, no such luck!

After the Genya Ravan session, Eddie Tuduri and I cut some songs for studio guitarist Jerry McGee at Sound City Studios in Van Nuys as well as some demos for Rosemary Butler, background vocalist for Jackson Browne, Ray Charles, and Kenny Loggins. Several weeks after these sessions were completed, I received a call from a singer named Kent Dubarri.

Dubarri, with his partner Gary Dalton, had recently finished their debut album on Columbia Records, and were preparing for a national tour. Dalton & Dubarri were signed with Shiffman & Larson, a superpower Hollywood firm that managed the careers of Loggins & Messina, Poco, Dave Mason, and many others. I agreed to meet them at Studio Instrument Rentals in Hollywood for an audition.

Dubarri was a stocky black man in his mid-thirties, a singer with the gift of gab, while Dalton, a few years younger, was a tall white guy with an outlaw's mustache who sang and played guitar. I was ushered into a large rehearsal room, and to my dismay, there was no Hammond organ in the room, only a piano. I tried to explain that I was an organ player, not a pianist. This fact seemed insignificant to Dalton and Dubarri.

Guitar in hand, Gary Dalton began playing his songs. The tunes sounded easy until I tried to accompany him on the piano. The key signatures sounded strange, and I wondered if my piano was out of tune. Dalton explained that he tuned his guitar from the key of *D-flat* (guitars are usually tuned from the key of *E*). He said that he wanted to get lower tones from his instrument. Consequently, all of his songs would be in the most difficult (and seldom used) keys in modern music, the keys of *D-flat*, *G-flat*, and *B*. Absolutely dreaded keys for pianists and organists because they require unfamiliar fingering patterns. Killer keys!

I found a pencil and paper and wrote down the chord changes for several songs. I played as best I could, while Dalton played guitar and sang. Both Dalton and Dubarri were grinning from ear to ear. I thought my playing was mediocre and sloppy, but they thought otherwise. I was puzzled. My silent question was answered by Dalton who said, "We've auditioned eighteen keyboard players, and you're the only one who can play in *D-flat!*" I was put on a small retainer of about $250 per week in today's currency and we spent the next several weeks rehearsing. Several of Dalton and Dubarri's songs required me to play a Hohner Clavinet, which was rented for me to take on tour. Best known for Stevie Wonder's riff on "Superstition" with its funky, growly sound on the low-end bass notes, the instrument was a favorite with musicians and audiences at the time.

Due to the difficult key signatures, I couldn't have much freedom as a soloist. I had to create and memorize my solo parts. Playing memorized solos is the antithesis of creative and meaningful improvisation. Under normal conditions, when I take a solo I have no plan in mind. The solo guides itself, forms itself, and completes itself. This is the true art of jazz, blues, and meaningful rock music. But with Dalton and Dubarri, I was forced to play in such terrible keys that I had to contrive my solos and relegate them to memory.

After Dalton and Dubarri had completed their search for musicians, our band included guitarist Allen Kemp. Allen had played with Rick Nelson and the Stone Canyon Band and had a gold record as lead guitarist on Nelson's hit "Garden Party." Allen and I soon became good friends.

Our first gig was at Doug Weston's Troubadour in Hollywood, where we were scheduled to share the bill with Nick Ashford and Valerie Simpson. A review in *The Los Angeles Times* called Dalton & Dubarri

"Excellent singers with a *top-notch band.*" After reading this review, Dalton and Dubarri began to show their true colors. In order to keep the band in its place, they laughed and called us "The Top-Notchers." There was nothing friendly or funny about this. It was a deliberate attempt to demean us and almost led to a fistfight between Allen Kemp and Kent Dubarri.

In spite of wearing keyboard-handcuffs by having to play in ridiculous keys, my playing was appropriate and according to published reviews, enhanced the band. As we musicians began to gain confidence, Dalton and Dubarri began to worry. After our closing performance at the Roxy Theatre on Sunset Boulevard, we were happy to hear the audience applauding as we entered our dressing room. Kent Dubarri would immediately turn our joy into anger and dismay. As if he were a drill sergeant he said, "Don't get the wrong impression. We are *not* a band. We will never be a band! You're just *street* musicians!"

Guitar player Allen Kemp wasn't a big man, but he had a strong disposition. Allen had played concerts worldwide, including one at Madison Square Garden with Rick Nelson. He had shared an apartment with Randy Meisner of the Eagles and accomplished more in music than any of us. Calling him a "street musician" pissed him off. Red-faced, he leaned toward Dubarri, pointed to his jaw and said, "Let me tell you something. You're full of shit!" When Dubarri didn't strike, Allen grabbed his guitar and left the dressing room. Dubarri yelled, "You'll be back. You've got nowhere to go!" Allen slammed the door, but he *did* return to the band. Major label tours were important and offered the opportunity for better jobs with well-known bands.

Our first big concert was opening for Rod Stewart and Rory Gallagher at the University of California at Santa Barbara's football stadium. When we arrived at the university, the beauty of the campus impressed me. Elegant palms, umbrella trees, and manicured lawns lined the curving streets. As we turned onto a road that led to the stadium, the campus police stopped us near a barricade marked "Artists Only." Our driver flashed a stage pass, and the barricade was pulled aside.

A gigantic bandstand had been constructed at one end of the stadium. At both corners of the stage were monstrous black speaker cabinets, rising almost twenty feet into the sky. At one corner of the stage was a full-sized sound console, manned by a professional engineer.

The engineer's sole task was to balance the sound for the musicians onstage so they could hear drums, bass, and themselves on monitor speakers. In front of the stage, about fifty feet from the band, sat another engineer. His job was to control the sound that blasted from the gigantic speakers to the audience. I had played large concerts before, but they were nothing like playing U.C. Santa Barbara — 16,000 fans packed the bleachers, while at least 5,000 stood on the football grinder. Over 20,000 people!

Dressing room trailers were parked behind the stage. Our band's trailer was furnished with platters of cold cuts, loaves of bread, bags of potato chips, and a cooler filled with Heineken beer. The food and drinks were included in our contracts for every gig we played in America, and we were given the same treatment as the stars, although our pay was meager, about $400 per week and $25 *per diem* for food in today's dollars.

Fans had come to U.C. Santa Barbara to hear Rod Stewart and Rory Gallagher while our band was new and unknown, but they enjoyed our opening set, which was well rehearsed and professional. People were crammed so close together that they had to applaud above their heads. After each of our songs, thousands of arms reached into the air, hands slapping. From the stage, their arms looked like the tentacles of friendly octopi. By this time, I'd learned that it was easier to play for large crowds than small audiences. The energy of the big crowd works like a magnet, flowing through the musicians while the energy of the musicians flows back to the crowd. We feed off each other in a way that cannot be described in words. It's *real*, it's wonderful, and beyond definition.

Our next gig was at Bill Graham's Winterland in San Francisco. We were booked for two nights, opening the show for the Steve Miller Band and Dave Mason. I decided this would be a good time to fly Anne and her mother up to San Francisco. My Scottish mother-in-law, Annie Wallace MacBeth, was quite a character. Only five feet tall, her blood still boiled with the "Brave-Heart" of her ancient ancestor, Sir William Wallace. Born and raised in Scotland, she retained a wonderful Scottish brogue. My nickname for her was "MacGregor," and she was about to make an unforgettable impression upon some of America's biggest rock stars.

When we took a taxi from our motel to Winterland, I didn't realize the significance of the theater. Only later would I learn that it was almost a second home to The Grateful Dead, Jimi Hendrix, and The Band. With an egotistical flash of my stage pass, I escorted my wife and mother-in-law through the artists' entrance. We were led upstairs to a large room with a pool table and TV monitors hanging from the ceiling. The monitors were connected to cameras that focused on Winterland's stage so that we could watch other acts as they performed. When bands weren't performing, the monitors showed a screen with ever-changing psychedelic images. Bubbles, expanding starbursts, kaleidoscopic flowers, and rainbows.

I entered a dressing room marked "Dalton & Dubarri" and met with the band. Looking in the mirrors that covered an entire wall, I made sure my hairstyle was "cool" enough for the audience of San Francisco hippies. I didn't realize that most of the flower children didn't know what the "hippie thing" meant any more than I did. They were just a bunch of kids trying to be nonconformists by conforming to one another.

I left our dressing room and was introduced to Bill Graham, Steve Miller, Dave Mason, and Graham Nash (of Crosby, Stills, and Nash). I took this opportunity to introduce Anne and her mother to these stars of rock music. By this time, my mother-in-law had drunk a few beers and her rather uptight British personality had become jovial and fearless. She noticed that Graham Nash and Dave Mason were smoking a beer can! Not the least intimidated by their fame, wee sixty-eight-year-old MacGregor walked up to Nash and Mason. In her Scottish brogue she asked, "What ye smokin'? Can I try a wee bit o' that?" Graham Nash handed her the beer can. MacGregor inhaled some smoke, grimaced, and said, "I dinnae like the taste o' this thing." She handed the can back to Nash. The musicians got a real kick out of MacGregor, especially when they watched her dance a few steps on the Highland Fling.

In the morning, we flew back to L.A. to prepare for our national tour. I was about to play the most important arenas in America, if not the entire world.

Chapter 20

Loggins & Messina, The Doobie Brothers

Joe Walsh, The Beach Boys, Little Milton, Dave Mason

Dalton & Dubarri's managers, Todd Shiffman and Larry Larson, also managed Loggins & Messina, who were at the peak of their popularity, packing every concert with thousands of fans, anxious to hear "Your Mama Don't Dance." We were scheduled to open the show on their 1973 concert tour of America. As a result, we had a ready-made audience at every gig, and success was ours to win or lose. To be more precise, it was up to our "leaders" Dalton and Dubarri to sell their songs to the public.

After we played our first concert at Concordia College in northern Minnesota for a crowd of about 6,000, we were driven to Minneapolis where we performed at the Metropolitan Sports Center for over 15,000 Loggins & Messina fans. Next came performances at Dane County Coliseum in Madison, Wisconsin, Northern Illinois University, Post College on New York's Long Island, and the list goes on. We played so many large arenas and auditoriums that we considered crowds of under 10,000 to be small-time gigs.

Although I didn't like pop music, I was somewhat in awe of Kenny Loggins and Jimmy Messina. They were close to being superstars and exuded a vibe of professionalism, confidence, and magical perfection. To other members of our band, I affectionately called them "Weasel and the Shuffler." Onstage, Jimmy's face resembled a weasel and Kenny Loggins, less serious but young and amazed at his own success, stood beside him, shuffling his feet.

Personally, Dalton & Dubarri's material wasn't to my taste. It was overly funky with chicken-strut rhythms that didn't appeal to rock audiences. Our performances were tight and professional, but lacked the excitement of straight-ahead rock 'n' roll. A few songs managed to groove enough to get audience response, and we occasionally received an encore, but customers had bought tickets to hear Loggins & Messina, not some unknown band called Dalton & Dubarri. After performing at the Syria Mosque Auditorium in Pittsburgh, our next gig would be at Madison Square Garden. I wasn't a bit afraid of playing the "Garden"; I just wanted to see New York!

As a child in California, New York City seemed like a magical place, a dream city in the distant clouds like the land of Oz. As a traveling salesman, my father often sent me postcards of the Empire State Building and other Manhattan landmarks. I remembered looking at pictures of New York on my Viewmaster, a plastic stereoscope popular in the fifties. I dreamed of someday seeing that great city of skyscrapers. When our plane flew toward the "Big Apple," I was sitting next to guitarist Allen Kemp. Whenever I saw a big city through my window, I eagerly asked, "Is that New York?" Allen just smiled and said, "You'll know it when you see it!" He'd already played New York with Rick Nelson at the infamous "Garden Party," but I could tell Allen enjoyed my newcomer's enthusiasm.

Allen was right. I recognized New York City when I caught my first glimpse through the window of our plane. It was a cloudy day, and I strained my eyes to see the Statue of Liberty, the Twin Towers, and most important of all, the Empire State Building. As the plane descended toward La Guardia, I filmed our landing with an old 8mm-movie camera.

From the airport, we were driven to the McAlpin Hotel on Broadway. My main concern was to visit the Empire State Building, but because of a tight schedule we were told not to leave the hotel. Not to be deterred,

Allen and I sneaked outside, hailed a cab and quickly arrived at the mythical monument of my childhood. We took an elevator to a height beyond my comprehension, then another elevator to the Observation Tower. I looked down at the streets of the city and became dizzy. Cars resembled plastic toys, and people looked like ants. I took a few snapshots with a cheap Kodak. Many months later, I discovered that one of my pictures was exactly the same shot taken by my father, twenty years earlier. Both pictures reside side by side in my scrapbook.

Allen and I rushed back to the hotel just before our band was about to leave for a soundcheck at the "Garden." All bands, (or their proxies if they're on the superstar level), need to do soundchecks before major concerts so that the soundmen can adjust audio levels for onstage monitor speakers and the vast audio system for the audience.

The show starred Loggins & Messina, Dave Mason, Poco, and our band. It was Thanksgiving Day, and the concert promoters arranged turkey dinners for us in a section of the Garden called The Rotunda. This area featured The Garden Club restaurant, complete with linen-covered tables and tuxedo-clad waiters. Allen and I took a table next to Dave Mason and members of his band. I admired Dave's music and wished he could hear me play Hammond organ. He might have offered me a much better job, but at that moment I was too hungry to talk business!

We were served tiny plates of turkey, stuffing, and mashed potatoes that were more like hors d'oeuvres than dinners. I wondered if meager portions were supposed to be "high class" in New York. The small amount of food on my plate made me angry. "To hell with class," I thought, and ordered a second dinner, followed by a third! Thanksgiving is supposed to be a feast! Our waiter looked somewhat annoyed and impatient, but I was hungry and insistent. Most of the musicians at our table had to eat three or four turkey dinners to satisfy their appetites.

As showtime neared, we left the restaurant and found our dressing room, located below the main arena. When it was time to open the show, I was excited and felt a rush of adrenaline. Like racehorses at Santa Anita, we musicians were chafing at the bit. We wanted to make music. The power of the crowd was overwhelming, and to compensate I asked a roadie to bring me two Heineken beers, which I chugged down like water. Otherwise, my playing might have been too frantic.

Looking at the audience from the wings, I saw thousands of faces. Not only were all of the seats occupied, but the entire floor was packed with fans. I later learned that attendance exceeded 22,000 people. The lights darkened, and stagehands led us to our instruments with flashlights like ushers at the movies. We were careful not to trip over the spaghetti-network of wires. Taking my seat at the piano, I tried to see the crowd but all I could see were vague shadows. Suddenly, almost-blinding spotlights ripped into my eyes. I was blinded and saw only blackness. A vast emptiness. Eventually, I could see people standing near the stage. Only when the spotlights panned the audience could I see the crowd. Thousands of faces from the floor to the sky.

This was the most important gig of my life, but I felt I was being punished for some forgotten sin. If ever I could show my talent as an organ player to the world, this was the time and place. If I could have played Hammond B3, I would have been able to impress the big-name musicians and their managers who were waiting in the wings.

Photographers and writers from major magazines and newspapers were there. Stars like Dave Mason and Kenny Loggins were watching and listening. Great jobs could have been in the offing. Musicians must be *better* than good to gain respect from stars, but sadly I was relegated to playing piano and Clavinet in the most difficult of keys. I might have been "good" on those instruments, but never "great." I needed a Hammond B3.

During our performance, we played a song that required a rock-style piano solo. I was seated at a Steinway Grand at stage left, near the audience. The piano was equipped with an expensive state-of-the-art audio pickup called a Helpinstill. During my solo, I heard the ear-splitting shriek of feedback from the stage monitors. I realized the Helpinstill had fallen on the piano strings! The piano went silent, as soundmen turned off my amplifier. I was in the middle of a solo, and the piano was dead! I must have deserved lots of bad karma, because this was the worst thing ever to happen to me on stage. Of course, it had to occur at Madison Square Garden.

White-hot spotlights were still focused on me when the piano broke down. Thousands of people were watching. My mind flashed with an idea: *"The people are watching but not really listening to me, there's so much sound coming from the band."* With this thought in mind, I back-kicked the piano bench. It went flying across the stage, almost hitting so-called star Kent Dubarri. Next, I fell to my knees and beat on the keyboard like Jerry Lee Lewis, fully aware that nobody could hear a note. I beat that piano so hard that people began to applaud. They thought they were hearing music, but it was all an illusion. And it worked! It even fooled the critics from *Billboard*, *Cashbox*, and the *New York Times*.

Two weeks later, we were booked with The Beach Boys at the Boston Music Hall in Massachusetts, an old opera house and home to the Boston Philharmonic. Giant, impressive pillars supported the balcony and surrounded the majestic stage. It was the type of auditorium where elegant old ladies of long ago peered at the stage through gold-plated opera glasses. It seemed almost sacrilegious for The Beach Boys to perform there.

During soundcheck I saw my friend, drummer Eddie Tuduri. He was on the road as The Beach Boys' drummer because they needed a *real* drummer in addition to Dennis Wilson. Eddie gave me a hug and said, "Congratulations, Rick!" Confused, I asked, "Congratulations for *what*?" Eddie replied, "Man, didn't you see the review in *Billboard* magazine? It said you 'took the show' with your piano solo at Madison Square Garden!" I told Eddie that nobody could hear the piano, and the whole thing was a fake. He was amazed at how literally tone deaf critics could be.

We left Boston the next morning to open for Loggins & Messina at the Norfolk Scope in Virginia, and then on to Constitution Hall (The D.A.R. Hall) in Washington, D.C. After our performance, we returned to the Howard Johnson Hotel across from the infamous Watergate complex. It was from our hotel that E. Howard Hunt and G. Gordon Liddy conducted their electronic surveillance of the Democratic National Headquarters in the Watergate, leading to Nixon's resignation. At this hotel, I helped save our guitar player from bleeding to death.

Allen Kemp and I bought beer at the Watergate, but our bass player and drummer bought tequila. After returning to our hotel room, we heard the sound of smashing glass from the room next door. Curious, we left our room to see what had happened. When our bass player opened the door, we felt the icy blast of winter wind. Looking inside, we saw a large hole in one of the windows. The bass player looked at us with twisted eyes and said that he had thrown an empty tequila bottle through the glass.

Walking down the aisle, Allen took a swing at a plastic exit sign. The sign shattered, as did Allen's right hand. Blood ran down his arm like crimson water. What could we do? Our bass player had smashed an expensive hotel window, and Allen had smashed the exit sign. I guided Allen back to our room and tied a towel around his arm to stop the bleeding. I knew he needed a doctor, but wondered how I could find help without being caught by hotel management. I devised a plan. First, I knocked on Dalton and Dubarri's door and said, "Allen cut his hand, and I need money for a doctor!" Dalton gave me $100 and I called a taxi company with instructions to meet us in front of the hotel. We couldn't take the elevator because it stopped in the lobby where Allen's bloody hand could be seen by hotel employees, so we climbed down several flights of stairs to an exit door. Outside, we met the cab that took us to Georgetown University Hospital. It took almost two hours for the doctors to repair Allen's hand. When we left the hospital, his bandaged hand looked like a white boxing glove.

Returning to our room, I grabbed the bloody towels I'd used to treat Allen's hand and threw them out the window. The sun was beginning to rise, and I watched the towels flutter to the roof of a nearby building. That might have been a good hiding place, except for the fact that it was winter. The roof was covered with snow, and the blood-stained towels shined like neon lights. We closed the curtains and escaped the hotel before the maids started their morning rounds.

The following night, we had a major gig with the Doobie Brothers at The Spectrum in Philadelphia. Dalton and Dubarri had no pity on Allen, his hand wrapped in a wad of bandages. Allen managed to wedge a guitar pick between his fingers and played for nearly 20,000 people without missing a lick. During the show, I noticed that his bandages were turning red. I think our leaders were hoping he'd fail, but Allen proved them wrong. He was always more professional than our employers, despite his occasional craziness on the road.

The Doobie Brothers were more fun to work with than Loggins & Messina. Their music was great, and they didn't project egotistical attitudes. The Doobies were down-to-earth nice guys. When we played the Spartan Coliseum in Little Rock, the Doobies invited us to their dressing room to share their beer. The promoters had forgotten to supply us with food and drink, so the Doobies came to our aid. We drank beer together and were treated as equals. In 1973, Michael

McDonald was not yet a member of their band. Once again, the face of destiny turned against me. The Doobies liked me, but they never heard me play Hammond organ. If they'd heard me play, I might have been offered the gig before McDonald came along. We played several more concerts with the Doobies and the Marshall Tucker Band before returning to play Winterland in San Francisco with Canned Heat, who had the hit record "Goin' Up the Country."

Our next gig was to open for The Beach Boys and Joe Walsh at the Long Beach Arena. (Joe Walsh was to "take the show" with his great song "Rocky Mountain Way.") This was our only large concert in the Los Angeles area, and I was happy that Anne could attend the show. On our way into the auditorium, I decided to show her a trick I'd learned from the road. I said, "We're going to walk right past the guards. We are going to enter this building without showing any ID or stage passes. Just act like a star!" We walked to the rear of the stadium and saw policemen blocking the musicians' entrance. They looked ominous with their black uniforms and guns, but we weren't intimidated. We simply stuck our noses in the air, refused to acknowledge their presence and walked past them as if we owned the place. The cops didn't say a word, and politely escorted us to our dressing room.

Our last gig with Dalton & Dubarri was at the CBS Records Convention, held at the Sheraton Hotel in Nashville. We boarded a chartered American Airlines jet in Los Angeles, filled with CBS executives, secretaries, and musicians. As is the case with most large corporations, the convention was basically a big party for CBS executives and employees with entertainment provided by some of their artists.

When our plane neared Nashville and prepared for landing, we found ourselves in a violent thunderstorm. Lightning was flashing, the plane was bouncing and passengers were praying for their lives. Sitting to my right, next to the window, was a young black woman. I assumed she was a CBS secretary. While the plane was attempting to land through the storm, the drinks on her tray flew toward the ceiling. She was terrified; her hands locked together in shaking fear. I looked out the window and saw a lake. I asked the girl, "What's all that water down there?" She whispered, "That's Old Hickory Dam." Then she pulled down the window curtain and said, "I don't want to see you, Old Hickory Dam! Oh God, please don't let us land in you. I don't want to land in Old Hickory Dam!" I thought this was so funny that I wrote a song about the incident.

The chorus goes, *"Lord don't let me, please don't let me, land in Old Hickory Dam!"*

The plane managed to land safely in Nashville, and the pilot received a round of applause from all on board. From the airport, we took taxis to the Sheraton Hotel. Over the next two days, we were treated to an exaggerated Tennessee flair of hospitality, with barbeque ribs, bluegrass bands, and clog dancers at a park on the outskirts of town. The barbeque sauce was so tasty that I sought out the person who'd made it. True to character, he was a fat hillbilly clad in overalls. When I asked if I could buy a bottle of his barbeque sauce to take home to California, he replied, "By God, this here's my secret recipe, but I'll sell y'all a jug for only $50!" He must have thought I was a rock star from CBS, and I declined his generous offer. To this day, I haven't figured out how he made such great barbeque sauce.

When it came time for us to play at the convention, our performance wasn't impressive. Not that the band didn't play well, but our "star" singers were too nervous to make a good presentation. Maybe they were afraid of the CBS executives in the audience, but whatever the case, the great blues singer Little Milton took the show. He burned our "stars" to the ground, and they knew it. In the dressing room, Dalton and Dubarri informed us they were going to cut a new album, using studio musicians instead of our band. Dubarri's last words were, "We'll call you when we need some street musicians."

Despite the cruelty of our employers, I feel fortunate to have toured with Dalton & Dubarri. We traveled over 36,000 miles in the United States and played for tens of thousands of people over a period of three months. It was an episode in my life I'll never regret, and it made my ninety-four-year-old grandfather proud. I'll never forget taking him to see his dentist. When the doctor greeted him in the waiting room, Grandpa pointed to me and said, "That's my grandson, Rick. He's a musician. He's played at Madison Square Garden!"

Chapter 21
Delaney and Bonnie

Delaney and Bonnie Bramlett were two of the most influential people in my musical life. In 1969–70, they'd heard me play with Blue Rose Band when we traded sets at The Brass Ring Club in Encino, and when I heard that they were looking for a new organ player, I felt certain I'd get the job. Auditions were set up at Studio Instrument Rentals in Hollywood.

When I entered a rehearsal room filled with other organ players, I spotted Chuck Morgan and thought, "Damn, Chuck is their drummer." Chuck and I had worked together in Blue Rose Band, and after the group broke up, I decided to continue working with Chuck's archenemy, guitarist Terry Furlong. Because of this, Chuck developed an unrelenting, irrational hatred toward me.

I took a seat on the sofa and listened as a slew of organ players auditioned. A musician always knows if he can play as well, if not better, than other players and I knew I could outplay *all* of the organists at the audition. I was the only *real* B3 player in the room.

I had paid my dues in South Central L.A. and Watts, in clubs most organists wouldn't dare to tread. When it came my turn to audition, Delaney asked me which song I would like to play. Immediately I said, "Only You Know and I Know," Delaney and Bonnie's current hit.

After I finished playing, Bonnie followed me to the hallway. As she was reassuring me that I'd get the job, I heard Chuck Morgan talking to Delaney, saying "Rick plays too busy!" and other negative comments about me. I didn't pay much attention to Chuck's negative words, because Bonnie was on my side. She gave me a hug and said she wanted me in the band. When I left the studio, I saw a piece of paper on my car window—a traffic ticket! While auditioning, the parking meter had expired. I put the ticket in my pocket and drove home to El Monte. Even though I was sick with the flu, I was filled with confidence and joy. Bonnie said she'd call the next day.

I stared at the telephone on our kitchen wall as if it were a time bomb ready to explode with good news. One day passed, then another. Whenever the telephone rang, I ran to the kitchen with the greatest of hopes, but after several days my hopes turned to dismay, sorrow, and anger. I realized I was being ignored. I began to face the fact that, for the first time in my life, I had lost an audition. Delaney and Bonnie had turned me down. I remembered Chuck Morgan's negative comments, and later would learn that Delaney paid close attention to his band members' attitudes toward new musicians. Delaney wanted his band to be happy, and abhorred dissension. Even though I played better than the other organists, Chuck had bad-mouthed me out of the gig.

Within a matter of months, Delaney and Bonnie's marriage ended in divorce. They went their separate ways, never to work together again. This considered, I didn't lose much more than pride. D&B were on the verge of superstardom together, that "fabulous couple" who were so great that Eric Clapton joined their band as a sideman. No matter how good they were as individual artists, their music as a team was matchless. With the slam of a judge's gavel, their winning formula for superstardom was lost forever.

Almost two years later, Delaney's guitar player Kent Henry called to tell me that Delaney was auditioning organ players for his new band. I liked Kent. He had played with Steppinwolf and Genesis, and we had a good chemistry both musically and personally. But ill feeling from Delaney's past rejection still lingered in my mind, and I was reluctant to audition.

Kent tried to encourage me, saying that Delaney had just signed with MGM Records and that his new album was sure to be a hit. I was between gigs, my backstabbing nemesis Chuck Morgan was no longer in the band, and I decided to give Delaney another try. There remained the possibility of failure, but show business is an endless path of rejection, and those who enter therein must learn to walk the bitter road.

I arrived at Delaney's Rock 'n' Roll Ranch in Sunland, California, and looked for a place to park my car. Many organ players were already there, eager to work with the legendary singer/guitarist. Delaney's home was impressive, located on several acres for his collection of prizewinning thoroughbred horses. The main house was a white ranch-style structure with several outbuildings including horse stalls, tack rooms, and a large cabin near the swimming pool where Delaney slept. In the main house lived Delaney's mother, Iva (Mamo) Bramlett, and his daughters, Michelle, Suzanne, and Bekka.

Connected to the house via a carport was a building that had been converted into a rehearsal room. Filled with microphones, amps, drums, a Hammond B3, and other equipment, auditions took place in this room. I stood on the gravel-covered driveway and listened as other organ players did their best to impress Delaney. Some of them sounded passable, but none stirred a feeling of competition in my heart. When my turn came to play, I took the audition seriously, wanting to prove my worth to Delaney. This time, he listened to my playing without the negative words from Chuck Morgan. He took me outside to the driveway, shook my hand, and said, "You're hired!"

Working with Delaney was both fun and educating. As most musicians know, he was an artist whose talent bordered on genius. The father of Southern gospel rock, Delaney grew up in rural Pontotoc, Mississippi, only twenty-six miles from Elvis's hometown of Tupelo, and like Presley, he was raised a Southern Baptist, often singing in the church choir. Also like Elvis, Delaney loved black music, especially the blues. Unlike Elvis, instead of mixing blues with country music, Delaney mixed blues and rock 'n' roll with the feeling of gospel music, thus creating something new. His influence spans the globe.

Under Delaney's direction, our band became tight, solid, and exciting. Before we recorded our first album, we played some interesting gigs at Knott's Berry Farm in Buena Park, where my grandparents had taken me as a child, and Rio Hondo College near my hometown of Whittier, which overlooked Rose Hills Cemetery. From the outdoor stage, we could see bereaved relatives watching their loved ones' caskets being lowered into the ground as we played our rock 'n' roll. In New Orleans that would have been a good "send-off," but not in Whittier.

We played the Palomino Club in North Hollywood, where country acts like Hank Williams, Jr. and Willie Nelson performed. Members of Elvis Presley's band came to hear Delaney, and some of them sat in with our group. Drinks were free, and I got so drunk that I grabbed a telephone book, ripping out the pages and throwing paper wads into the audience. Our entire band was drunk, and the redneck crowd didn't know what was happening. After the gig, I spotted a cluster of tall bamboo near the parking lot. I broke off a stock of bamboo about twenty feet long, stuck it out of the window of my car, and drove down Lankershim Boulevard. My intention was to give the bamboo to my wife, but it fell onto the street. Luckily for me, the police were nowhere to be seen. The cops were busy at the Palomino, trying to quell a redneck riot that broke out after our last set.

At the Whisky a Go Go in Hollywood, we were headliners over the Spencer Davis Group, who had the hit, "Give Me Some Lovin,' " when Stevie Winwood was in their band. I had always wanted to play the Whisky and was excited about the gig. On the afternoon before our performance, we went to the club for a soundcheck. As the soundmen adjusted our audio levels, guitar player Kent Henry fell to the stage and went into convulsions. Flat on his back, Kent's body reverberated in a frenzy, like an out-of-balance washing machine. As the soundmen watched, thinking this was part of our show, I realized Kent was having an epileptic seizure. I ran to the stage and stuck a drumstick between his teeth to keep him from biting his tongue. Next, I ran outside to where I remembered seeing a fire alarm, pulled the lever on the red box, and soon there were firemen and paramedics on the scene. Kent was taken to a nearby hospital, where he recovered in time for our show. Our band received rave reviews from the local press, and if Kent had experienced another "fit," the reviews might have even been better!

I recorded five albums with Delaney over the next three years, including one for MGM, released under the title, *Giving Birth to a Song.* Although the album contained several potential hits like, "So Much in Love With You Baby" and "Nothing Without You," MGM didn't promote the album and it went nowhere. It was the same story with the second album, which we recorded for Motown. Produced by Jimmy Bowen and Ray Ruff, this record (and its never-released follow-up album) allowed me to record with some of the greatest studio musicians in America, including guitarists Steve Cropper, (Otis Redding, Wilson Pickett, The Blues Brothers), my friend Don Preston, Jerry McGee (Kris Kristofferson), and Nashville guitar maestro "Thumbs" Carllile. Our drummers were Jim Keltner (Bob Dylan, Elvis Presley), Stu Perry, and Ringo Starr, who later overdubbed his drums. James Jamerson (bass player on almost every Motown hit, including "My Girl") and Chuck Rainey (Marvin Gaye, Aretha Franklin), took turns playing on various songs. The Ikettes, background singers for Ike and Tina Turner, along with a string section from the L.A. Philharmonic and one the best horn sections in Hollywood completed the lineup. To top this off, Delaney's vocals were soulful, unique, and powerful. But it was all for naught. As with MGM, our Motown recordings were never promoted. The only aspect of the music business I fully understand is how to cut good records, and I have no idea why MGM and Motown didn't make an effort to sell these albums. But the fact remains that without the special combination of both Delaney and Bonnie, neither managed to record a hit as solo artists.

Four years later in 1978, I received a telephone call from Bonnie Bramlett offering me a job in her new band. I had always admired Bonnie's singing on "Soul Shake," "Only You Know and I Know," and especially "That's What My Man is For." She was the best white female soul singer I'd ever heard. She and Delaney had played all over the world, including Carnegie Hall, Madison Square Garden, and Royal Albert Hall in London. Bonnie was such a gifted singer that, at age fifteen, she was hired by Ike Turner to be the only white member of his famous "Ikettes." For this job, Bonnie had to wear a black wig and apply dark makeup to her face to pass for black.

We began rehearsing in Hollywood and I was put on a weekly retainer of about $500 in today's dollars. When I rolled my electric piano into the rehearsal hall, Bonnie became upset. On one side of my piano's flight case was a "Delaney Bramlett" sticker. One of Bonnie's roadies asked me to hide Delaney's name, so I turned the case around so that his name faced the wall.

Cajun music star Doug Kershaw was organizing a band in another room at the same rehearsal facility, and Doug often visited our room to listen to Bonnie and our band. I was impressed by the multiple talents of Kershaw and his Cajun fiddle and accordion playing. Doug and Bonnie shared the same management company, which almost got me fired at an unhappy later date.

Bonnie was signed with Capricorn Records, home of the Allman Brothers, the Marshall Tucker Band, and others. She had recorded a new album titled *Memories* in Muscle Shoals, Alabama. Our job was to tour America on a bus to promote this record. I had never been on a bus tour and was warned that it would be tedious and painful. (My previous national tours had provided flights for long distances.) Our lead guitarist, Ricky Hirsch (formerly with "Wet Willie"), almost refused to go. He told me of the misery that was in store on a bus. Nevertheless, I wanted to work with Bonnie and nothing could dissuade me.

Before the major U.S. tour began, we were booked to play some gigs in California and Nevada to "get our act together." After playing a show in Bakersfield, we were driven to Lake Tahoe in a Winnebago to play the Cal Neva Lodge. As usual, I became sick with the flu as soon as I left home. By the time we reached Tahoe, I was too sick to get out of bed. Unable to eat solid food, soup was my only diet and feverish sweat drenched my body. I felt worse than dead, and was worried about my ability to play.

Our bass player, Robert Wilson, took pity on me. He came to my room and offered me a little white pill, an amphetamine, which I had sworn off many years earlier. As sick as I was, I accepted the drug. Robert warned me, "Whatever you do, don't snort any coke after you take this!" I foresaw no problems, since I never liked cocaine.

Before our show began, it seemed that our dressing room was all mirrors and snow. Someone had brought a bag of cocaine, and the straw was passing from one musician to the next. In a stupid effort to be "one of the boys," I snorted some coke along with the rest and started to feel awake, stoned, and crazy.

When we went on stage, I was blitzed from the cocaine. I took a microphone and yelled, "Rock 'n' Roll in Lake Tahoe!" The audience remained silent. We began playing our songs, and when it came time for my organ solo, I went completely nuts. To over-compensate for my stupefied condition, I tried to show off. I sat on the keys of the organ, creating a sound that was musically correct but infuriated a redneck roadie from our opening act; the organ belonged to a member of his band, Pure Prairie League. After our show, the roadie grabbed my shirt and threatened to "kick my ass." I wasn't used to roadies insulting me. They usually *kissed* ass, not kicked it! It took one of our roadies to control the angry cowboy.

After the gig, I was wide awake from the coke and amphetamine. The Cal Neva Lodge was a casino, and the floor was covered with crap tables, slot machines, blackjack dealers, and roulette wheels. Thinking myself to be a master gambler, I decided to play blackjack. It took me several hours to lose the $200 I had in my wallet. In the meantime, members of our band begged me to stop gambling, but I wouldn't listen. After I lost all my money, I began to write worthless checks to buy more gambling chips. I was sure I would win back my losses and cover the checks. When I continued to lose, I accused the dealers of cheating. They became so angry that they called a security guard. When all was over, I had lost $700. Of this amount, $500 was from worthless checks. Suddenly, I began to worry about the Mob. The Cal Neva was an infamous hangout for Sinatra, his "Rat Pack," and their Mafia buddies.

I called home to my eighteen-year-old daughter Kelli and told her the Mafia was going to kill me. I knew Kelli had a savings account from her waitress job at Bob's Big Boy restaurant in Sunland, California. I also knew she loved my Appaloosa horse named Breeze. I told her I'd sell her the horse for $500. She agreed, and put the money in my checking account before the Cal Neva checks bounced. I guess this saved my life, and my daughter later made a profit when she sold the horse. Some people lose their shirts in Las Vegas. I lost a *horse* in Lake Tahoe, and nearly lost my job as well.

From Lake Tahoe, we bounced in the Winnebago to San Francisco. I thought I had done a great job with Bonnie at the Cal Neva, and covered my foolish gambling debt. Still sick with the flu, I went to bed. Later, I grew hungry and ordered a pizza. While trying to eat, I heard band members Ricky Hirsch and Al Kaatz entering their motel room, adjacent to mine. I heard one of them laugh and say, "Rock 'n' Roll in Lake Ta-Ho." Upon hearing this, I put a drinking glass to the wall and heard Ricky saying, "He's living in the past!" Then I heard Al Kaatz answer, "Yeah, but he plays good!" Ricky responded, "I wouldn't know. I can't hear him on stage."

That was enough for me. I felt humiliated and defeated. If I had been suicidal, I might have killed myself. Instead, I pretended not to know what the musicians were saying and called Bonnie's room. I told her I was sick and needed to go home and rest. I took a taxi to the San Francisco airport and flew to Burbank, near to my home in Tujunga, California.

As I was recovering at home, something sinister was happening behind my back. Our band was scheduled to fly to Denver the following week to begin a national bus tour. I was eager to make up for my mistakes in Nevada, but several days passed without hearing from the band. Little did I know that during this time, Bonnie and her manager were trying to replace me. I was kept in the dark, thinking that she and the other musicians were my friends. When I learned that Bonnie was trying to fire me, my first impulse was to quit. I was hurt and very angry. However, I needed to regain my self-respect. I needed to prove that I was a good musician. I felt like a dirty, filthy thing, crawling through the slime. Once again, drugs had brought me to the bottom.

Bonnie's manager called me for a special meeting at his home in Beverly Hills. He explained that the Cal Neva Lodge had threatened to cancel all of his contracts, due to my behavior at the blackjack table. He said that he'd looked for a solution (another organist) but "the answer was me." I didn't get to keep my job because he liked me or thought highly of my playing. It was because he couldn't find anyone to take my place. There wasn't enough time for another organist to learn Bonnie's show.

I agreed to be a good boy and continue with the tour. No one stood up for me; not one of my "friends" explained *why* I went nuts in Nevada. All the bass player needed to do was say, "Rick was sick and I gave him a "white" to help him make it through the gig. I warned him not to snort any coke, but he snorted some anyway, and that's what drove him crazy. He doesn't usually act like that." Instead, he remained silent and left me hanging in the wind.

I decided to fight back. Like crawling off the floor of the Pomona jail in 1968, I needed to rise above the muck and regain my self-respect. I agreed to complete the tour with Bonnie, not because I liked her singing but because I needed to stop hating myself. The only way I could accomplish this was by playing organ as well or better than anyone else in rock music. I set out to prove this in over thirty states and Canada.

Chapter 22

Bus Tour with Bonnie Bramlett
My Road to Redemption

In April of 1978, I arrived at Los Angeles International Airport with Bonnie and my "pals" in the band. We boarded a plane for Denver and were scheduled to play a gig at a club called The Blue Note in Boulder before our bus tour began. Unlike other tours when I'd played with opening acts, this time I was in a band with star billing.

The Blue Note was packed with Bonnie's fans. Before she came on stage, we played Jimmy Smith's "Chicken Shack," which featured my organ. My chops were hot, and I was determined to redeem myself to Bonnie and the band, but mostly to myself. It only takes one or two great performances to remind musicians that you're an important part of the group. I intended to stand them on their heads and prove I could match or outplay any organist in rock music.

When playing concerts, whether in vast arenas or small showcase nightclubs, the most important songs are the first and the last. The first song has to be strong and exciting enough to make the audience yearn for more, and the last song is how you'll be remembered.

Bonnie knew this well, and opened her Colorado show with a song written by Delaney titled "Living on the Open Road." It was straight-ahead rock 'n' roll and got the crowd fired up for more music. Then Bonnie sang songs from her new album, which was the real purpose of our tour. Good songs, yet songs the audience hadn't heard before. Fans always want to hear an artist's hit records, so Bonnie interlaced familiar songs into the show, such as "Superstar," which Delaney and Bonnie wrote with Leon Russell and was recorded by The Carpenters. Delaney and Bonnie's version couldn't get airplay because it included the lyrics, "*Sleep* with you tonight," while the Carpenters' lyrics were changed to "*Be* with you tonight." We closed the show with Stevie Winwood's great song "Can't Find My Way Home," which gave me a chance to show off on organ with lots of Bach-like runs in the intro and earned us an encore.

Bonnie sang the show with the soul of a gospel diva, and our band played strong and solid behind her, but as the first set neared its *finale*, we began to feel dizzy from the mile-high Colorado altitude. Our drummer, Big John Thomassie, nearly fell over backwards on his drum stool. His 300-pound body slammed against the wall behind him but he managed to literally "bounce back" from the wall and finish the set. During intermission, the club owner brought an oxygen tank to our dressing room. We took turns inhaling the pure oxygen and began to feel much better. In fact, we started feeling a natural high.

Our second show was like musical fire on stage, and we received several standing ovations. Although I was still recovering from the flu, I played my parts as close to perfection as possible. I was on the road to redemption, and the band was aware of my performance. I left the stage with my head held high. I had regained my self-respect. Walking to the dressing room, I was given many compliments and asked to sign several autographs. My bandmates were aware of this, and I thought, "So much for firing Rick Allen, you bastards of betrayal."

The venues we played with Bonnie were theaters, outdoor festivals, and mostly showcase clubs. Although Bonnie was a "name" artist, she didn't have the drawing power to play huge arenas without Delaney. There would be no gigs like Madison Square Garden on this tour. But what I refer to as "showcase clubs" were important gigs, with professional soundmen, people to control the spotlights, and emcees to announce the acts.

The morning after our gig in Boulder, we were introduced to our touring bus, an old silver coach that had once driven country stars from Nashville. The smell of Diesel exhaust filled our lungs as we stowed our luggage in the storage compartment. Upon entering the bus, we were greeted by walls of ugly, brown Naugahyde. Cracked and faded with age, there were Naugahyde seats in the front, a Naugahyde-covered icebox replete with Bonnie's Perrier water, and a Naugahyde chair for our driver. To complete the front compartment was a padded, Naugahyde-covered room with a faded star on the door for Bonnie and her miniature dog.

Walking past the front area of the bus, we opened some faded paisley curtains to see our sleeping area. My first impression was the vile odor of Lysol from the toilet. The stench was enough to bring tears to our eyes. The beds were actually racks, similar to those in jails, installed in bunk-bed fashion, one on the bottom, another above. I immediately chose a bottom bunk, and put my carry-on luggage on the Naugahyde mattress. I closed the paisley curtains and returned to the front of the bus.

My claiming the bottom bunk would eventually get me into an argument with guitar player Al Kaatz. Slow to claim a bed, Kaatz was forced to sleep in the bunk above mine. The bus was hot, and the closer to the ceiling, the hotter it became. Al complained to me, saying "How come you get the bottom bunk?" My answer was simple: "First come, first serve." I was about ten years Al's senior, and had suffered enough in the music business. I staked out my claim, and there I would sleep for the entire tour. There was a blacked-out window beside my bed with vents at the bottom that blew a constant blast of hot air. Bonnie wanted to keep the bus *hot*, but I couldn't stand the heat. I solved this problem by covering the vents with silver duct tape.

Many funny things happened on that bus. The first incident occurred after we left Colorado and headed east. While driving through Kansas, we ran out of beer! This was a major travesty. Rolling down the Interstate, I told our driver we needed to stop for some brew and asked to use his CB radio. Surely truckers in the area would know where to buy beer in semi-dry Kansas.

The driver, a man called "Joplin," handed me the CB microphone, I clicked the button and politely asked, "Does anyone know where we can buy some beer in Kansas?" I released the button and awaited an answer.

The airwaves remained a hiss of static. No response. I tried once more, asking the same question. Still no answer. That was when the driver said, "Hey man, they'll never answer you if you talk like that! You have to sound like a redneck." Taking his cue, I clicked the microphone button and said with a twang, "Hey, good buddy. Do y'all know where we can git some beer 'round these parts?" Instantly, a trucker answered my call. "Hey, good buddy," he said, "just take the Abilene exit, turn left at the second signal, and you'll see a gas station that sells beer." He was right. We took the exit, bought some beer, and stored it in our Naugahyde-covered icebox next to Bonnie's Perrier water.

The next crazy incident happened somewhere in New England. While driving to Boston on the Interstate, our driver made CB contact with the driver of an eighteen-wheeler ahead of our bus. He told the driver we wanted to pass his truck. As the big truck pulled to the right lane, we got a good look at his rig. It was beautiful and clean, with a pure white cab and polished chrome. So far as trucks go, it was top of the line. The proud driver was polite and cordial. Just moments after we passed the white truck, something outrageous happened.

Our drummer was using the bathroom at the back of the bus. When he finished, he saw a large red handle next to the toilet. Half drunk and thinking that the red handle would flush the toilet, he turned the lever, emptying gallons of human waste upon the highway. The brown sludge immediately splashed onto the front of the beautiful white truck. Our driver got a call on the CB from the trucker. "Hey," he said, "Your bus just shit all over my rig!" As our driver apologized, we caught a glimpse of the truck in our rearview mirrors. His windshield wipers were going fast, and the entire front of his truck was covered with sewage. I still feel sorry for that trucker. Lesson to be learned: never follow a busload of crazy musicians!

After playing cities and towns all across the U.S., it came time for us to play New York City at the famed Bottom Line in Greenwich Village. It would be my third experience playing New York and my second engagement at the Bottom Line, this time in a band with "star" billing. I not only loved playing the Big Apple, but took New York gigs very seriously. New Yorkers are accustomed to hearing the best musicians on the planet. They're very critical and hard to please. As Sinatra sang, *"If you can make it there, you'll make it anywhere!"*

The Bottom Line was packed with Bonnie's fans, including rock star Stevie Winwood, who was sitting directly in front of me. When we played his composition "Can't Find My Way Home," I played an intricate organ intro. Stevie is an organ player, and I wanted to show him what I could do on Hammond. As the song began, Bonnie said over the microphone, "Eat your heart out, Winwood!"

Our show at the Bottom Line was broadcast live on a New York radio station and professionally recorded. I was given a cassette of our first show and thought it sounded great! Live recordings are usually better than studio albums because they capture the excitement of both the musicians and their audiences. Years later, I sent a cassette copy to Bonnie and suggested she release it as an album. Bonnie didn't like the recording and said if I had it released, she'd take legal action. Of course, I had no intention of releasing the album. Although my playing was on the tape, it was Bonnie's concert. She should have taken my advice, because a bootleg version is currently being sold in Japan. Our performance at the Bottom Line can also be heard on the Internet.

Our drummer, "Big" John Thomassie, was a New Orleans masterpiece. Half Cajun, half Italian, he was the best "pocket" drummer I have ever known, solid and soulful. Big Johnny was also a fantastic cook and the craziest good-time coonass I have ever met. Johnny could both "stir up a roux" on the stove and stir up a crowd of thousands with his music. I don't believe that a better drummer has ever walked this earth. But, as I said, Big Johnny was crazy. There are stories about Johnny that are funnier than words can say, stories that stretch from coast to coast.

Johnny looked more French than Italian. With high-arched eyebrows, a black beard and weighing over three hundred pounds, he resembled a French-Canadian lumberjack, but his mannerisms were entirely New Orleans. Johnny's voice was a raspy growl, somewhere between Louis Armstrong and Dr. John. He was unique and authentic.

One insanely funny incident occurred at a hotel in Tulsa, Oklahoma. By sheer and somewhat ironic coincidence, our band was staying at the same hotel where a Catholic priest was being elevated to the position of bishop. This was a very important event to the Catholic clergy, and our hotel was filled with hundreds of priests.

Big Johnny, bass player Robert Wilson, and I entered an elevator to find it packed with young priests dressed in black vestments with liturgical collars. Big Johnny, a disillusioned Catholic, began to laugh. In a friend- ly way, he pinched the collar of a priest and growled, "Hey, priest-ess, do you wanna smoke some weed?" The priests were taken aback and as- tonished, as Big Johnny repeated the question. By the time we reached our floor, some of the priests yielded to temptation and followed us to Big Johnny's room.

The sight was hilarious. Big Johnny rolled a joint and passed it to the nearest priest. He took a long hit, then passed the joint to another priest. The room filled with the burning-rope odor of marijuana as Johnny and the clergymen took deep inhalations, coughed, and asked for more. Some priests sat in chairs while others sat on the floor, all getting high. I didn't like marijuana and wanted to buy some beer, but Oklahoma had strange drinking laws. It was Sunday, and the priests told us it was im- possible to buy alcoholic drinks. Even the bishop couldn't buy brandy. "How," they asked, "can *you* get beer if the bishop can't buy brandy?"

Determined to buy some beer, I asked one of the priests to drive me around Tulsa. His car was typical of so-called religious people: light brown in color with black-wall tires and tiny hubcaps. The priest drove us through the city until we spotted a small shop that advertised beer. He kept the engine running while I entered the store and bought a case of Budweiser. As we drove back to the hotel, we each downed a can of Bud. The priest was glad to have some cold brew, and I realized he was basically a normal guy who probably didn't believe half of what he preached. When I asked him why the Catholic Church teaches things that aren't in the Bible, he answered "We give people what they want to hear." Pretty cool for a priest.

Upon re-entering Big Johnny's smoke-filled room, the congregation of stoned priests began to applaud! Big Johnny yelled, "Hey, look at Rick Allen! He got beer when your bishop can't get nothin'!" We shared the beer with the priests as they continued to take hits of weed. Thumbs and forefingers to their lips, they smoked just like weed-heads in California.

One night in Pennsylvania, I heard someone pounding on my door, and Big Johnny stumbled into my room. He slammed himself down on my bed and said, "Man, the band wonders about you! They *axed* me, 'Why don't Rick Allen act like us?' and I toll 'em, 'Rick Allen's a gentleman!'" Big Johnny continued, "I respect you for that, Rick Allen. My daddy was a gentleman too. You be like my daddy. My daddy was a Mason.

You and my daddy would've got along good."

What a switch in opinion! I had been transformed from the crazy speed-freak gambler in Tahoe to being a "gentleman," apparently considered by some band members to be a flaw in character. I still don't understand what the problem was. I drank beer with the boys and laughed at their jokes. Was my use of decent English aggravating the band? After all, they were intelligent guys and weren't close to being rednecks. Were they jealous of my playing and thought me arrogant? Was it because my IQ was above freezing? I guess I'll never know the answer to this weird situation.

I remember an incident that happened in the restroom of a hotel in Oklahoma. One of our roadies with the appropriate name of "Gleek" was standing in front of the mirror while I was washing my hands. He said, "Can I get you a warm towel, sir? Would you like a fresh bar of soap, sir? Let me know if there's anything you need, sir!" I took all this in stride as appropriate behavior on his part, never dreaming that he was being sarcastic and patronizing. Maybe I have too much British blood in my veins to have realized that he was insulting me!

When we drove south to Memphis and stayed at the Holiday Inn, Big Johnny's family drove up from New Orleans with an ice chest filled with boiled crawfish. All members of the band were invited to Johnny's room to feast on this Louisiana delicacy. Big Johnny dumped the fragrant crawfish on a coffee table, and those of us who had never been to New Orleans were somewhat confused. We were told to "pinch the tails and suck the heads." I didn't mind eating the tails, but refused to suck the heads. I thought they might contain pieces of brain, although they only contain spicy juices from the boiling process. We took some crawfish to our separate rooms on paper plates.

For those who've never eaten crawfish, they are small crustaceans, somewhat like mini-lobsters. The only edible part is the tail, and the rest must be discarded. Boiled crawfish are bright red in color and smell of garlic, spices, and onions. After the shells, heads and claws are discarded, they begin to reek like dead fish. Our band occupied ten rooms at the Holiday Inn and when we finished eating crawfish, we put the shells, legs, and whiskered heads into our trash cans, placing them in the hallway. Some of these cans tipped over, spilling dead crawfish bodies in the aisle. The odor was overwhelming, as other hotel guests tiptoed around the reeking exoskeleton remains.

I returned to Big Johnny's room just in time to catch the fun. When I walked through the door, I noticed that his carpet was flooded with water. I quickly learned that instead of putting his crawfish heads into a trash can, he had tried to flush them down the toilet, causing it to overflow. I will never forget Johnny's telephone call to the front desk of the hotel. He picked up the telephone and yelled, "Hey! Get me a plumb-ah!" We were almost evicted from the hotel, and Big Johnny began taking my place as the troublemaker in the band.

Our next gig was in Georgia, and I decided to take a break from the bus and fly to Atlanta and spend the night at a Holiday Inn. The next day, I boarded a Greyhound bus toward the Allman Brothers' farm near Juliet, Georgia, to meet up with Bonnie and the band.

The nearest town to Juliet on the bus route was Forsyth. The road was a state highway, and the Greyhound stopped at every little town en route. I had been to the South many times, but not the Deep South. When the bus driver announced each town we entered, I couldn't understand his accent. The only way I could identify the little towns was by reading signs on the roadside. As other passengers listened to the driver announce their destinations, I stared out the window, looking for clues. After several hours, I heard the driver say something like "Sythe." Outside the bus, I caught a glimpse of a sign that read "Forsyth." I left the bus and called Bonnie, who was staying at Dickey Betts's cabin on the Allman Brothers' farm. She asked me to wait for her at the main intersection of town.

This was the redneck part of Georgia, reminiscent of the movie *Deliverance*, and my presence drew attention from the townsfolk. It wasn't because of my Levi's and T-shirt, that were common in Forsyth. What caused people to stare was my hair, which was combed into a huge Afro, like Sly Stone or Jimi Hendrix. Also, I was wearing an expensive leather coat and black Florsheim boots. As I sat on my suitcase waiting for Bonnie, people stared from trucks and dusty cars. Soon Bonnie arrived in a pickup truck. Her first words were, "Hey Rick, you look like an L.A. rock star!"

As Bonnie drove toward the little town of Juliet, I asked "Is Juliet near the Allman Brother's *Ranch*?" Bonnie immediately corrected my Western grammar. "Farm!" she said. "Ranches are called *farms* in the South." When we reached the little town of Juliet, Bonnie stopped at a small grocery store. She needed some Perrier water, and I wanted some beer. Before we entered the store, Bonnie taught me another lesson about 1978 Georgia.

"When you get your beer, walk up ahead of the blacks," she said. "That's the custom here. The blacks will step aside." I objected, saying I was not prejudiced against black people. I entered the store, grabbed a six-pack and walked toward the cashier. Several black people were waiting in line, and as I walked toward the counter, they moved out of my path like submissive sheep. They allowed me to reach the front of the line, not because they thought I was some sort of rock star, but because I was *white*. I was embarrassed and felt great shame.

When we arrived at the Allman Brothers' farm, I was astonished by its size. Bonnie said it was close to 1,000 acres. We drove past several cabins, houses, and trailers, all of which belonged to various members of the Allman Brothers' Band, as well as roadies, drivers, and stage crew. Down a narrow dirt road and past a lake we drove until we reached Dickey Betts's A-frame cabin. Dickey was on the road with the Allmans, and I was disappointed. I had been looking forward to confronting Gregg Allman in an "organ duel."

I spent the night sleeping on a sofa in Dickey Betts's cabin while Bonnie slept upstairs in the loft. Big Johnny was passed out in a kitchen chair, his head on the table. I awoke early, and decided to take a morning stroll. I left the cabin and began walking up a dirt road toward a small lake. It was a beautiful spring morning and I could hear the tree-tapping of woodpeckers and the melody of an early-morning mockingbird. I fell in love with the South all over again, and I was anxious to tell my wife about Georgia. Suddenly a sound sent terror throughout my body. The thunderous barking of huge dogs.

From where I stood on the dirt road, I could see two gigantic Great Danes. They had stopped barking and were on the run, running toward me! As the dogs rounded the lake, I ran for my life to the cabin. With beasts at my heels, I managed to slam the door before they reached their prey. Within seconds, the dogs were on the porch, barking and scratching at the door. Bonnie ran down from the loft and began to laugh. "Those dogs won't hurt you!" She opened the door and told the dogs to "Go home!" The dogs trotted gleefully away back to their side of their lake.

"What happened?" Big Johnny asked as he awakened from all the commotion. When I told him, both of us were afraid to leave the cabin. To make our escape, Bonnie drove her pickup to the front yard as Big Johnny and I made a mad dash and jumped into the back.

With the Allmans' song "One Way Out" in my mind, the dogs chased us until we reached a main highway and rode to the safety of a Holiday Inn in Forsyth.

The next day, we went to Little Richard's hometown of Macon, and had a rehearsal at Capricorn Records. This was the studio where most of the Allman Brothers' famous hits were recorded, and the acoustics were great. Gregg Allman's B3 was a powerhouse in itself, beefed-up to play loud and nasty. The rehearsal was for our next gig at the Great Southern Music Hall in Atlanta. Phil Walden, President of Capricorn Records, wanted us to make a good impression in his home state. In fact, he invited President Carter and his family to attend our show.

When we arrived at the Atlanta gig, we found the parking lot scattered with men in black suits. Inside the club, we encountered more of these men. We wondered if they were deaf, because they all wore hearing aids. After a few moments, we realized they were Secret Service agents. President Carter wasn't able to attend but sent his son "Chip" to see our show. Chip's presence was to honor Bonnie and Phil Walden for helping with Carter's presidential campaign.

After the show, Chip was waiting in our dressing room, surrounded by Secret Service agents, all wearing "hearing aids," their faces like masks of stone. Chip said he loved our show and drank beer with us. After being assured that the Secret Service wasn't interested in enforcing Georgia law, some musicians lit up "joints." Chip didn't smoke any marijuana, but it seemed strange that members of our band could smoke dope in front of government agents. These special cops worked for the President and his family. They were like guard dogs, protecting their masters, and Chip's safety was their only concern. I never got to play for the President but drinking beer with his son was good enough for this kid from Whittier!

Chapter 23

Bonnie Bramlett Tour Continues
New Orleans, Houston, Los Angeles, Vancouver, B.C.

The day after our gig in Atlanta, we boarded the bus and began the long eight-hour haul to New Orleans. I had always wanted to play in that famous music city. As a boy, my first improvised piano boogie was the New Orleans anthem, "When The Saints Go Marching In." New Orleans music was in my soul from the beginning, almost as if in a past life I'd been a piano player on Bourbon Street. Sometimes I wonder if that might be true!

Our bus rumbled on until we finally crossed the Louisiana state line. Excited, I looked out the window, expecting Louisiana to be beautiful like Georgia with plantations, trees draped with Spanish moss, and picturesque bayous. Instead, I saw miles of treeless marshland and a gray sky reminiscent of smoggy Los Angeles. This was not the Louisiana I had expected to see. I didn't realize that only a few miles to the north were endless acres of pine trees, beautiful bayous, and ancient moss-draped oaks. When the bus pulled to a stop at our motel in Gretna, a suburb of New Orleans, I was overcome by the ninety-plus-degree heat and the sweltering humidity. Water condensation from the motel's air conditioning poured steadily off the roof like a wide open garden hose, splashing on the asphalt parking lot. I felt like I was being steamed alive, like a lobster.

After cooling off in my room, bass player Robert Wilson took me on a tour of the French Quarter, just across the Mississippi River from our motel. We parked our rental car and walked to Jackson Square. I was amazed to see so many artists, mimes, fortunetellers, and clowns on the wide sidewalks. There were quaint shops along the way, selling everything from *gris gris* to antique furniture. The appetizing aroma of gumbo, shrimp étoufée, jambalaya, and other delicacies filled the air. As we walked toward Bourbon Street, I told Robert that the French Quarter couldn't be *real*, that it had to be a reconstruction of bygone days like a Hollywood movie set. Robert laughed and said, "No, Rick, this is the real thing!" I didn't believe him. Still simmering with a low-grade fever from the flu, the Quarter took on a surreal, dreamlike quality like the world of illusion experienced from taking peyote. We entered Pat O'Brien's bar where I drank a Hurricane, a very strong drink made with rum, but I was so overwhelmed by the Quarter that the drink barely calmed my nerves.

When we reached Bourbon Street, the wonderful smell of New Orleans cuisine was quickly replaced by the stench of rancid beer turned sour in the gutters from hundreds of almost-empty plastic cups. Novelty shops, striptease clubs, hustlers, panhandlers, barkers, and drunken tourists jammed the broken sidewalk. Young black boys were tap dancing in the street, doing head-over-heels flips. There were small cardboard boxes on the pavement to collect tips. I tossed a dollar into a box and was immediately approached by three black boys. "Hey Mister," the tallest boy said. "Bet I can tell where you got those shoes at!" I was wearing black Florsheim boots I had purchased in Glendale, California. I thought there was no way the boy could guess "where I got my shoes at." I agreed on a bet for one dollar. Bass player Robert told me to forget the gamble, but I insisted on playing the game. I held the dollar in my hand and said, "OK, tell me where I got my shoes at!" The boy answered, "You got them on the sidewalk on Bourbon Street in New Orleans!" He took my money and I learned a lesson.

As we walked up Bourbon toward Canal Street, I heard a blend of music I had never heard before. Dixieland, Zydeco, and the "lift up my soul" sound of the blues! I was drawn to the blues like a dog to raw meat. It was coming from the Old Absinthe Bar at the corner of

Bourbon and Bienville Streets. The Old Absinthe was a New Orleans landmark, the walls covered with faded, yellowing business cards, some printed in French. Robert explained that the old cards weren't meant for business, but for introduction. Some had been exchanged between French "gentlemen" who wanted to kill each other in duels.

On stage was Brian Lee, an almost-blind white man playing blues guitar. His voice sounded black and his playing reminded me of Albert King. Even though I was playing with Bonnie Bramlett, an international star, I would rather have been playing blues at that little club. I was both physically and emotionally sick of traveling all over America, and would've been much happier playing blues in New Orleans. I thought that Dixieland jazz was the musical mainstay in the "Big Easy," but learned that the blues was even more popular with tourists. After a plate of red beans and rice at Buster Holmes' restaurant, we returned to our motel on the West Bank of the Mississippi. The following night, our show with Bonnie at Ole Man Rivers' in Gretna went without incident and I finally got a good night's sleep after the gig.

The next day, we boarded the bus and rode for over five hours to Houston for our next gig at a club called Steamboat Springs. For the first time on Bonnie's tour, the club owner reneged on our contract and refused to pay us *before* the show. He wanted to pay us after the show, which is an age-old way of cheating entertainers. We musicians wanted to take the night off, but Bonnie insisted that we play. She was the "star" who customers had paid to see, and she made it clear to the audience over the microphone that we were being ripped-off and were playing "for free." We played two shows in Bonnie's spirit of *"The show must go on!"*

At Houston, after over 25,000 miles of misery on the bus, Bonnie's management granted us clemency and flew us to Seattle, Washington, for our next gig at a large club on the outskirts of town. After the show, I spent my first sleepless night, lying in bed waiting for the sun to rise. Eventually, there came a knock on my door, and I climbed into a rental car headed for Vancouver, Canada. We had two rental cars, one for Bonnie and the girl singers, another for the musicians. As we neared the Canadian border, our car radio was playing "Werewolves of London," and some of us sang along with the funny song. "How-ooo, Werewolves of London, How-ooo." I looked out the window and saw a sign that read "Welcome to British Columbia." Big Johnny saw the sign and shouted, "Yeah, man! Columbia!" thinking of the South American mecca of marijuana.

When we attempted to cross the Canadian border, the immigration cops made us pull into a special parking area. We were told to enter a small building, where we were systematically searched and interviewed. Our pockets were searched, our suitcases were searched, as well as the letters and envelopes in our briefcases. We were a bunch of long-haired American musicians with work visas, and the cops were trying to bust us for drugs. We were drug free, but ironically one of our roadies had stashed a bag of marijuana in the trunk of Bonnie's car, which easily crossed into Canada without inspection. To the border guards, it was just a carload of innocent girls.

Vancouver, B.C., was the most beautiful city I'd ever seen. Clean and modern, it was surrounded by majestic snow-capped mountains and crystal blue waters from the Pacific. Quaint gas lanterns lined the streets, and the distinctive atmosphere of Great Britain was evident, from fish and chips and Union Jacks to Queen Elizabeth's picture on the currency. I remember thinking that Vancouver was as close to the United Kingdom I'd ever get, although many years later Anne and I were able to visit England and Scotland.

When we arrived in Canada, there was a beer strike in British Columbia. This was cause for panic, as we were beer drinkers and our favorite beverage was unavailable. The alternative was hard cider, which we quickly learned was a good substitute and relatively low in alcohol. We exchanged our cash for Canadian dollars and checked into a five-star hotel near the foot of Vancouver's Grouse Mountain where we were scheduled to play a rock festival. I remember Big Johnny throwing the Canadian money on his bed and saying, "Look at this shit! It looks like Monopoly money!"

There were only two ways of getting to our gig on Grouse Mountain: by mountainside tram or helicopter. When we left the hotel and climbed into a Lincoln limousine, we told the chauffeur to take us to the tram. Big Johnny and I brought some hard cider along for the ride, and this upset the chauffeur. He rolled down the window that separated us and said, "Drinking in a limo is against the law!" I told the driver to mind his own business and pushed the button, closing the window between us. We were part of an all-star package that included Jimmy Buffett, Martin Mull, and Hoyt Axton. I could have dealt with the cops in the unlikely event they stopped our limo.

We boarded the tram and headed up the mountain. I was afraid of the ride because our small enclosure hung from only one steel cable. It was still daylight and we could see rocks and snow below as the tram began to rise. Buzzing on hard cider, Big Johnny decided to have some fun. He grabbed a support rail in the tram and began to shake the little tramcar with his heavy body. Soon the tram was swinging from side to side. I feared it would fall off the wire and crash to the ground. I grabbed Johnny, begging him to stop, and we managed to arrive safely on the mountaintop. We saw the outdoor stage where we'd be performing and soaked up some of the beautiful alpine scenery before returning to the tram for a ride back down the mountain.

Our gig was scheduled for the following afternoon, after Hoyt Axton's performance. Again we took the limo to the base of Grouse Mountain, but this time I decided to take the helicopter instead of the tram. I had never flown in a helicopter and thought the flight would be fun. Robert Wilson warned me about the 'copter. He'd taken a helicopter ride at a Louisiana fair and was terrified. I should have heeded his words.

Robert and Big Johnny climbed into the back of the helicopter, and I was given the dubious privilege of sitting in front, next to the pilot. I felt a rush of excitement as the 'copter took to the sky, but my elation soon turned to fear. The front of the small helicopter was enclosed with clear plastic, and I could see the mountains beneath my feet. Robert began to laugh and told the pilot to "show off his skills." High over the Canadian Rockies we flew, but not high enough for me! The pines were getting dangerously close to the blades of the helicopter, and I knew what would happen if the large rotating blade hit a treetop. Beneath my feet, I could see glaciers and imminent death. Robert decided to increase my terror by asking the pilot to stop in mid-air and fly the 'copter backwards! I have never experienced more fear in my life.

Hoyt Axton was our opening act and I took an immediate dislike to the man. He seemed brutal, whiskey-drunk, and mean. A huge bear-like creature, he entered our dressing room with a star attitude. During his performance, Axton stopped his show in mid-song and pointed a finger at his drummer, Stu Perry, who was a friend of ours. In front of several thousand people, he told the drummer, "Play it right or you'll be walking home to L.A.!" Bonnie shouted, "Don't worry, Stu! We'll take you home!" Although Axton had written some big league hits like "Joy to the World" and "Never Been to Spain" recorded by Three Dog

Night, his show was boring and weak. When our band came on stage, we rocked the Canadian Rockies! Axton was musically "axed to the ground" by Bonnie and our band, and he had it coming.

After we returned to Los Angeles, I realized Bonnie had "forgotten" to pay me for our gigs in Canada, Seattle, New Orleans, and Houston, which amounted to two weeks wages, totaling $600 (about $2,000 today). The night before my grandfather's ninety-ninth birthday that we planned to celebrate at our home, Bonnie called me. She said she was going to "accept Jesus" and be "saved," coincidentally at her ex-husband Delaney's church in Sunland, California. She asked me to accompany her on piano the following morning while she sang some gospel songs. I tried to explain that the following day was my grandfather's birthday, but Bonnie insisted I play piano. She ended the conversation with the words, "Tomorrow will be payday, Rick!"

The church was located on Delaney's street, a few blocks from his home. I met Bonnie there, and we rehearsed some traditional hymns. When a small congregation entered, Bonnie sang "Amazing Grace" and "Just a Closer Walk With Thee." With her impeccable and soulful voice, that little church had never heard such great singing. Just Bonnie with me on piano was enough to blow the steeple off the roof. Perhaps Bonnie was "saved," but one thing for sure—she saved my money for herself. I waited for over a year before I was finally paid. Later in New Orleans, Big Johnny said he had never been paid and had given up on ever seeing his money.

Big John Thomassie, that great and crazy drummer, died from a heart attack in his mid-forties and went to an early grave. I attended his funeral in New Orleans and saw his body in a casket. There were drumsticks in his left hand. At the cemetery, a brass band played "The Saints" as Johnny's casket was placed into the family crypt. I kissed my fingers and touched them to his casket. "Good-bye, my friend," I whispered.

Chapter 24

Tragedy in Paradise

After the Bonnie tour, I was sick of traveling on the road. I was also sick of Los Angeles and the music business. Anne and I decided to buy a cabin in the San Bernardino Mountains. I was thirty-five years old and planned to sell mountain real estate while Anne found employment at a local bank. We spent our weekends in search of an affordable cabin in the mountain resorts of Big Bear, Lake Arrowhead, and Wrightwood before discovering the friendly little town of Crestline. It was both ideal and idyllic, with Swiss-styled storefronts and chalets, a pretty lake, and cabins within our price range. With the help of a Realtor, we found a nice A-frame cabin and began our mountain dream. Unfortunately, our dream would soon become a nightmare in paradise.

After we bought the cabin, tragedies began to occur within our family, as if by designed sequence. My dear grandmother Co, already suffering from Alzheimer's, fell and broke her hip. Her mental condition deteriorated after surgery, and she remained hospitalized for the remainder of her life. I loved my grandmother as if she were my mother, and seeing her in a nursing home crushed my heart, especially when she no longer recognized me. The pain cut me so deeply that my mind became numb to the actuality of her condition, like a disinterested third party. I suppose this was a natural mechanism to keep me from going insane with grief. Instead, I felt anger toward my grandmother for losing her mental faculties. My shame for those feelings will never rest. But I had to be prepared for another challenge: caring for my beloved one hundred-year-old grandfather.

My grandmother's hospitalization left him alone in his Santa Ana apartment. When I told Grandpa that Anne and I wanted him to live with us, he said, "You're taking on a big responsibility, Rick." There was no worry about responsibility in our minds. My grandparents had been my pals and guiding lights since I was born, and Anne and I loved them both almost beyond comprehension. But sadly, there was a great difference: my grandmother was no longer herself, whereas Grandpa was completely coherent and sharp-witted. The thought of placing him in a nursing home was never considered.

Anne and I organized a bedroom area for Grandpa on the main floor of our cabin, close to a heating vent to keep him warm at night. During the day, Grandpa sat near the cabin's sliding glass doors where he could see colorful mountain blue jays and big, puffy squirrels scavenge for peanuts on our snow-covered front deck. On winter evenings, I'd put some wood in our Franklin fireplace and set them ablaze. Grandpa loved to see the burning logs, and said the fireplace gave him a feeling of peace and comfort. He said, "Isn't it strange, Rick, how Fate has brought us together at this time of our lives?"

By the time Grandpa reached the age of 102, he was stricken with incurable cancer. We arranged the cabin like a hospital, with a wheelchair, bedside toilet, the rank smell of Lysol, and constant nursing care from my wife, daughter, and me. Although Grandpa's body was withered and failing, he never lost his wit.

Grandpa was having problems breathing, so I took him to a hospital in Lake Arrowhead where his diagnosis was determined to be pneumonia. His doctor met me in the hospital's parking lot and presented me with the most heart-wrenching choice of my life. He said, "You have two choices: let your grandfather die from pneumonia or let us treat his pneumonia and let him die from invasive colon cancer."

The doctor added, "From my experience, people with intestinal cancer suffer great pain." What a choice I had to make! I instructed the doctor to allow the person I worshiped more than anyone on earth to die from pneumonia. My mentor, my pal, my grandpa died that same night, and my inner tears will never dry. The next night, Grandpa came to me in an extremely vivid dream. Knowing I was interested in ultimate knowledge, he said, "It's like being on a river, Rick." Then Grandpa asked, "Will you be OK without me?" and I answered, "Yes, Grandpa, I'll be fine. You're free to let go."

There was a small nightclub close to our Crestline cabin called the Gregory Inn. Shortly after Grandpa's death, Anne and I went to the Gregory to hear a local band, and I made the mistake of drinking several gin martinis. As a beer drinker, I should have known better. I became sick and very drunk. When we left the club, the police were waiting at the door. Apparently, the bartender had called the cops because I was too drunk to drive, although he gave me no warning.

I told the cops we could walk to our cabin, and there was nothing to worry about. We weren't going to drive our car. That wasn't enough for the police. On the empty street in front of the nightclub, they said I was "drunk in public." They made me take a drunk test, just like a drunken driver. On a steep mountain road, the cops told me stretch out my arms and touch my nose. This maneuver caused me to fall over backwards, hitting my head on the pavement. Rendered unconscious, I was quickly awakened by the pain of a billy club, jammed lengthwise across my ribs. I was dragged to my feet and handcuffed. Barely conscious, I was driven to the San Bernardino County Jail and locked in the drunk tank. The cops didn't arrest Anne, and allowed her to walk home.

In the morning, Anne posted my bond and met me at the jail. As we rode back to Crestline, I realized I was having trouble with my vision. The trees and rocks appeared blurry and blended into a mass of green and gray. I also had the most horrendous headache I'd ever experienced.

The next day, Anne drove me to the emergency room at St. Bernardine's Hospital in San Bernardino. After a CAT scan, I was diagnosed with an epidural brain hemorrhage. I was placed on a gurney and rolled to the intensive care unit, with EEG and EKG wires attached to my head and chest for constant monitoring. It was a Catholic hospital, and compassionate priests and nuns often visited me, even though they knew I didn't share their faith. They may have thought I was about to die, but I never doubted my survival.

I was under the care of a wonderful neuro (brain) surgeon, who ordered daily CAT scans of my head. He said he might need to operate to remove the blood clot from the back of my brain unless it dissipated naturally. The risks of surgery included possible blindness, but my doctor was confident he could perform the operation successfully. I was coherent enough to refuse surgery as long as possible, and had an intuition not to eat salt. I had a feeling that salt might cause blood to coagulate rather than allow my blood clot to dissolve. However, I began to crave Mexican food and persuaded Anne to smuggle a burrito into my hospital room, which I ate with *mucho gusto*! Daily CAT scans began to show my blood clot reducing in size, and after ten days in ICU, my doctor had some good news. The clot was gone, and he ordered my release from the hospital. I asked him if I could drink a beer when I got home. His reply was, "Just so long as you don't fall on your head!"

While I was in the hospital, Anne had kept a terrible secret from me. She hadn't been able to reach her mother by telephone for several days and feared that something was wrong. While I lay in my hospital bed, Anne asked the Los Angeles police to enter her mother's apartment, where she was found lying dead on the living room floor. Afraid that this sad news might cause my brain injury to worsen, Anne bore her grief alone and I didn't learn of her mother's death until I was home from the hospital. When she needed me most, I was unable to give her the love and comfort she so desperately needed. Anne was incredibly brave to keep this news from me while I was in the hospital.

Thanksgiving has always been an important day for me. When I was a child, it meant going to my grandparents' house for the best meal of the year. My grandmother Co was an excellent cook and would prepare turkey, stuffing, cornbread, and many other dishes, although my favorite was always her delicious stuffing. My parents would say, "We're going to Co's house for dinner," and dress me up in a suit and tie for the happy occasion. On Thanksgiving Eve, 1982, our telephone rang in the middle of the night. The phone was close to Anne's side of the bed, and when she answered I could tell that my mother was calling. Since my mother had been visiting my grandmother at the nursing home in Ontario, it wasn't hard for me to grasp the reason for the late night call, but the reality didn't strike until I heard Anne say, "Honey, Co expired at two o'clock this morning." No matter her dementia, and no matter that death was better for her than her disorientated life in a nursing home, Co's passing was final and forever. Rational thinking couldn't stop my grief. Within one year, Anne and I lost three of our dearest loved ones. We were numb with grief. When our pain was at its worst, Anne made a decision. We would move to New Orleans and start a new life in music. She gave me a little note that said, "A chance of a lifetime in a lifetime of chance." I still carry that note in my wallet.

Chapter 25

New Orleans
Wayne Bennett, "Mighty" Sam McClain, C.P. Love

In March of 1983, we flew to New Orleans in search of a new home. I had taken Anne to the Big Easy before, and we had a general idea of where we wanted to live. We had spent the past three years in the mountains, and knew that north of Lake Pontchartrain in St. Tammany Parish there were endless acres of tall pines, which reminded us of Crestline. We wanted to find a house in the country within driving distance of New Orleans so I could commute to work once I found a gig. With the help of a gigantic real estate lady who was so fat that her Cadillac almost touched the ground when she sat behind the wheel, we put a deposit on a house in the little town of Bayou Lacombe.

After we returned to California, our daughter Kelli married her boyfriend and moved in with her new husband. At the same time, our son Craig was discharged from the Air Force, fallen in love with a girl named Joanne, and intended to marry her. Craig and Joanne decided to move to Louisiana with us, and start their life together in the Bayou State. We rented a U-Haul truck, loaded up our furniture, and hooked

Anne's Dodge to the back of the van. Craig and his fiancée would follow us in their compact car. We had two dogs: a black and white collie-mix named Brandy and a light brown pitbull called Fricket. Both dogs rode cross-country in the Dodge behind our van, and caused great interest to people who passed us on the Interstate. Fricket insisted on sitting in the driver's seat, directly behind the wheel, while Brandy sat to her right like a passenger. It looked like Fricket was driving the Dodge, and as we drove through the deserts of Arizona and New Mexico, people grabbed their cameras and took snapshots.

We arrived in Louisiana during the flood of April 1983 and slowly navigated through fender-high waters until we reached our new home. We found the house locked, and had to break a window to enter. It had taken us five days to drive from California. We were tired beyond exhaustion but still excited to be in our new home. Our half-acre yard was partially flooded, but the water didn't reach the house. Tall pines, a lone cypress, and two beautiful magnolia trees adorned the property. The sweet, almost overwhelming perfume of magnolias in bloom filled the warm, humid air. On our street, Spanish moss draped the ancient oaks like Christmas garland. This was definitely not California. Louisiana was a brand new life.

Music was our main objective in moving to Louisiana, and after an anxious night's sleep, we headed to the French Quarter. I was unknown in New Orleans, and had to start from scratch to build a name for myself. The only way I could accomplish this was by finding bands that would allow me to sit in on organ. I felt a strange mixture of confidence and fear. The confidence came from my years of experience in professional music, while my fear was of New Orleans itself. It was the birthplace of jazz and the home of the blues. Nevertheless, after a three-year sabbatical from music, I was determined to prove myself in this new city.

We walked up Bourbon Street until we reached the Old Absinthe Bar, the same club I had visited while touring with Bonnie Bramlett. On stage was the same guitarist, Brian Lee, cooking out the blues like a master chef. We entered, took a table, and waited for intermission. When the band took a break, I asked Brian if I could sit in with his band. I knew I could "burn" his organist, and was hoping for a job. I told Brian, who was trying to play like Albert King, that I'd worked with Albert in Los Angeles. I also told him I had played with Howlin' Wolf and Sonny Boy Williamson. This *braggadocio*, although true, was my first mistake. In Brian Lee's mind, I was either a liar or a conceited bastard. Where my experience would have been welcomed news to bandleaders in L.A. or New York, I didn't realize that New Orleans was comparatively "small time." My credentials made bandleaders wonder what I was doing in Louisiana. Why had I left L.A.? After a while, I learned to keep my past a secret.

After intermission, Brian announced my name and called me to the stage. The organ was like a wounded beast, held together with duct tape and equipped with a labyrinth of wires and strange attachments. I managed to find a setting that *almost* sounded like a Hammond B3. We began playing B.B. King's "The Thrill is Gone," and Brian took the first solo. After he sang another verse, he pointed to me. I took off with a powerhouse blues solo, and soon heard a crashing sound near the bandstand. A table, along with glasses and beer bottles, had been tipped over by some happy customers who were standing to applaud. When I finished my solo, there were cheers and whistles. A waitress came to the stage with a tray of cold beers for the band, compliments of the club owner. When I left the stage, I told my wife I had landed the gig!

During intermission, I went outside the club to talk with Brian Lee, expecting to be offered a job. I had torn the club apart with the organ. I was devastated and shocked by what he told me. He said, "You're very 'showy,' but you can't just walk in and take a gig because you're better than someone else. Those days are gone!" I felt both insulted and angry. Just as I had blown away his organ player, Brian Lee blew me away. Thinking back on this incident, I realize it would have been unfair of me to rob the other organist of his gig. I had been thinking back to earlier years in Milwaukee, when outplaying another musician was my only means of finding work. But Brian Lee had another reason for rejecting me, namely jealousy. Fate entered the picture when Brian's drummer, Kerry Brown, asked for my telephone number and said, "Hey, man, you upstaged Brian Lee. That's why he doesn't like you! He's an egomaniac, a legend in his own mind."

After a few days, Kerry Brown called me. He was putting a trio together with blues singer "Mighty" Sam McClain and wanted me to be part of the group. Kerry and Sam came to our house for a rehearsal, and we went over some blues songs such as Bobby Blue Bland's "Love Light" and "Stormy Monday Blues." I was impressed with their music. Kerry was a talented drummer with a New Orleans "street-beat" flair, and

Sam was a strong back-alley blues singer. He reminded me of "Blue" Bland. Both of my new friends were black, and Kerry asked if I was willing to play black clubs. I told him that black clubs were fine with me!

Kerry Brown was a man of many talents: drummer by night, embalmer by day at a local mortuary. He was also quite proficient in stretching the truth. Kerry told me our first gig would be at a club where Fats Domino played when he was in town. I believed him until I saw the club. It was called "Goose and Sons' Car Wash" and owned by Kerry's boss at the mortuary. To call it a dump would be an understatement. Located on an obscure corner in a dilapidated neighborhood, the tiny club was painted bright orange with "CAR WASH" in black letters on the front. It looked like it was ready for Halloween. Fats Domino would never have entered such a place, let alone performed there. I couldn't help thinking, "From Madison Square Garden to Goose and Sons' Carwash!"

I had never played a black club in the South, and needlessly carried a .25 automatic in my pocket on opening night. I wasn't aware of the lack of racial prejudice in New Orleans. The people at Goose and Sons' treated me like a friend and brother. Although the pay was only forty dollars per night, I loved playing that little club. The people liked my organ playing, and understood what I was saying musically. Soon we were offered another job at a club called The Hollow Point, where we were each paid sixty dollars per night. I was slowly climbing the ladder of success!

My goal was to be the best B3 player in New Orleans, and black clubs were both the hardest places to prove myself and the best places to build my chops. We billed our act as "The Crazy Rick Allen—Kerry Brown Trio featuring 'Mighty' Sam McClain." I made a few phone calls, and managed to have our names and upcoming gigs advertised for free on New Orleans radio station WWOZ and in the *Times-Picayune* newspaper. I used the word "Crazy" before my name to draw attention. This worked almost *too well*. Musicians all over town were calling me "Crazy Rick." They probably still do, but it accomplished my purpose: it made people take notice and remember me.

"Mighty" Sam McClain was an unpredictable alcoholic, sometimes happy and friendly, other times downright ornery and mean. One night after playing at The Hollow Point, Sam went crazy in the parking lot. Drunk on Taaka vodka, he wanted to fight with Kerry Brown.

Kerry was a skinny young man and could never have fought with muscular "Mighty" Sam. I talked Sam into entering my truck and drove to a late-night restaurant on Basin Street. As we dined on fried chicken, Sam told me he was about to become homeless. He was behind on his rent and was going to be evicted from his apartment. I didn't have much money, but wrote Sam a check for $100 to pay his weekly rent. After nearly a year, Sam repaid the loan, and I give him credit for this.

During this time, I was stricken with mononucleosis. I was sick for over three months. Every week, I lay in bed and although I'm basically an agnostic, prayed that I would be well for the weekend. My prayers were never answered, and every weekend I drove the 100-mile round trip to New Orleans and played the gigs for Sam. That was because Sam was broke and hungry, and needed the money to survive. I remember being so ill that I lost control on my truck. My Chevy Blazer began swerving on the Interstate, and I had to pull off the road to rest. Once I reached the club, I was too weak to unload my organ. As I sat at a table, dripping with cold sweat, Kerry Brown tried to unload my Hammond B3 by himself.

I heard a loud crash from the parking lot and stumbled to the door. There, lying upside-down on the asphalt, was my organ. The fall had broken off the wooden lid, and the Hammond lay on its back like a wounded soldier. Somehow we managed to carry the organ into the club. I got some nails from a bartender and hammered the lid back in place, but it was show time and the organ wouldn't play. Sicker than any dog could ever be, I removed the back of the B3 and found some disconnected wires. With the help of solder and a book of matches, I reconnected them. The club owner, Miss Jackson, was mad we were late, so we started playing immediately. During our first set, my organ bench collapsed in the middle of a song and I fell to the floor, hitting my head against a wall. Sam was still singing, and as I hit the floor, my hands never left the keyboard. Sam finished his song without my missing a note.

I felt responsible for Sam and loved him as a friend. Anne found a good job in the mortgage business, and I could have stayed home and gotten well. Instead, I came close to working myself to death. Covered with cold sweat, hands shaking, I went to work every weekend. Several years later, Sam moved to Boston where he was offered a high-paying job with a blues band. He quit drinking, became successful, and sent me a video of his life's story. In the hour-long video, Sam talked about his hard times in New Orleans with drummer Kerry Brown but never mentioned my name.

A little seventy-year-old tap dancer called "Pork Chop" (Isaac Mason), standing less than five feet tall, would come to The Hollow Point and dance to our music. He'd toss his hat on the floor and dance for tips. "Pork Chop" and I became friends and shared beers together in the parking lot. He would climb into my Chevy Blazer and take a seat, his legs so short that his feet couldn't reach the floor. "Pork Chop" was a real gentleman and a great dancer. Anne and I loved the little man, and upon his death I was honored to be a pallbearer at his funeral. The ceremony was held in a black church, but attended by people of all races. Little "Pork Chop" was a legend in New Orleans. A great big man in a little body.

I played over twenty black clubs in the New Orleans area with drummer Kerry Brown. Some with Sam, others with rhythm and blues singer C.P. Love, a Creole who sang like a mix between Sam Cooke and Wilson Pickett. A fantastic vocalist, he could sing Pickett's "I Found a Love" to absolute perfection, something few singers could accomplish. I continued to make sure our gigs were advertised over local radio and published in New Orleans' leading newspaper.

Kerry informed me that guitarist Wayne Bennett was looking for a gig. Bennett had been the lead guitarist for Bobby "Blue" Bland, playing on many of Bobby's hit records, including "Stormy Monday." Bobby "Blue" Bland was one of my childhood idols, and I thought it would be fun working with his former guitarist. But my first gig with Wayne would be a hilarious disaster.

Kerry booked our band at a little joint in Gretna called the Washington Bar. I had played Gretna before with Bonnie Bramlett at a club called Ole Man Rivers, but that might as well have been in another universe compared to the Washington Bar. Gretna is located across the Mississippi River from New Orleans, and the closer you get to the river, the more dangerous the neighborhood. There are housing projects in the area that would cause any driver, black or white, to roll up his windows and lock his car doors. Using a city map, I located the Washington Bar. Upon entering the club, I took a visit to the men's room. Inside, behind the restroom door, was a full-sized crap table. Men were gathered around the table, throwing dice and dollar bills on the worn and faded felt. They took no notice of me as I entered the toilet area. I had seen gambling in New Orleans before, but never in a restroom!

Kerry and I rolled my Hammond B3 into the club. There wasn't a bandstand, so we set up our equipment on the dirty faded-yellow linoleum floor. Wayne Bennett, guitar in hand and nose in the air, walked into the bar with the self-important flair of a maestro about to perform at Carnegie Hall. Our singer, C.P. Love, took my microphone, which was plugged into a guitar amplifier and we began our first set.

Our gig was in late December and someone in the audience requested "Please Come Home for Christmas" by Charles Brown, a traditional Christmas song in New Orleans. I had heard the song and felt I could "fake" my way through it. But when Wayne Bennett realized I didn't know *all* of the chord changes, he stopped playing his guitar in the middle of the piece while people were dancing, turned toward me, and yelled, "Hey, man, I thought you *knew* this song!" The dancers were astonished, and I was burning mad. Bennett took off his guitar, leaned it against the wall, and walked out the door.

During the break, we went outside for some fresh air. Standing on the broken sidewalk, I approached Wayne, my eyes on fire. Bennett was a big man, but I was angry. I pointed to a broken plastic Dixie Beer sign outside the bar and said, "Wayne, I don't care if you've played with 'Blue Bland.' I've played with famous people too. But now we're *both* playing in this dump. Don't you ever embarrass me in front of an audience again!" Bennett thought about my words and said, "I was wrong. I'm sorry. Will you accept my apology?" We shook hands and remained friends until his death in 1992.

After several months, fate would come my way in the form of "Mr. Mother-in-Law," the notorious Ernie K-Doe. I would finally get a chance to play the French Quarter. I thought there would be organists on Bourbon Street to compete with me, but there were none. I thought I'd make more money in the French Quarter, but for most musicians, it was less than I was making in the black clubs. However, with a "star" like Ernie K-Doe, I was back in my element. With K-Doe's notoriety, I was able to play important gigs and let New Orleans hear what I'd worked for all my life.

Chapter 26

Ernie K-Doe, "Mr. Mother-In-Law"

Pete Fountain, King Floyd,
Johnny Adams, Benny Spellman

I've always loved the song "Mother-in-Law" by Ernie K-Doe. When the owner of a local grocery store told me that K-Doe was opening a nightclub in our little town of Bayou LaCombe, I found it hard to believe. K-Doe was a major R&B star, and working with him would get me out of the ghetto clubs. No matter how much fun they were to play, I yearned for higher ground, namely the French Quarter. I asked the store owner where K-Doe's club was located and soon found myself at the Morocco Room.

I'd expected the Morocco Room to be a flashy high-class establishment. Pulling into the parking lot, I was astonished to see a dilapidated stucco building with sheets of faded blue paint peeling from the outside walls. It was even uglier than the ghetto clubs I'd played in New Orleans. With a degree of trepidation, I went inside and found a man and woman at work, the woman scrubbing the Formica tabletops and the man mopping the yellow linoleum floor—Ernie K-Doe himself.

"Mr. K-Doe, my name's Rick Allen and I play Hammond organ," I said, while shaking his hand. When I mentioned that I had worked with Etta James and Dr. John in Los Angeles, K-Doe appeared skeptical. I could almost hear him thinking, "If this guy's worked with those big stars, what's he doing here in the boondocks?" Realizing that music spoke louder than words, I invited Ernie to our house where I fired-up my Hammond B3 and played a few tunes. K-Doe grinned like the Cheshire cat. He said he'd never heard a white boy play like me, and was happy I had access to professional musicians like bassist Robert Wilson, drummer Kerry Brown, guitarist Danny "T," and saxophone virtuoso Tim Green. It was decided that we'd play for the grand opening of the Morocco Room as "The Burn K-Doe Burn Band."

Ernie K-Doe was the epitome of a New Orleans character. Flashy, wild, crazy, conceited, and unique. He had a radio show on WWOZ, a blues and jazz station in New Orleans, and began to advertise the opening of the Morocco Room. With screaming enthusiasm, K-Doe yelled, "Friday night at the Morocco Room in Lacombe, Louisiana, come see me, the Emperor of the Universe, with my Burn K-Doe Burn Band. That's at the Morocco Room, y'all, in Lacombe, Louisiana. Oh lord, we're so great I gotta kiss myself. *Burn K-Doe Burn!*"

Johnny Adams' biggest hit records were "Release Me" and "Reconsider Me," both recorded in the late 1960s. On opening night, he was sitting at a corner table wearing dark glasses, and I thought he might be blind. I knew of his reputation and was aware that he was both a great singer and an accomplished guitarist. He was *way* "out of place" in the Morocco Room and had agreed to sing as a favor to his friend, K-Doe. But Adams was a star and expected to be treated as such. He sat alone at a Formica-topped table, waiting to sing a few songs and go home.

When the clock struck 10:00 p.m., both K-Doe and I became anxious. The little club was packed, but we had no drummer. Johnny Adams was anxious as well, if not pissed off, and wanted to begin the show. There was a young kid in the audience who said he could play drums. In desperation, I let him play Kerry Brown's drums, which were still in the club after a rehearsal. The kid was far from professional, but managed to hold the beat while Johnny Adams sang a few songs. As Johnny was leaving the club, Kerry pulled his van into the parking lot. "Sorry I'm late," he said, "I had a wreck!" He took his seat at the drums, and K-Doe was able to perform his show with a real drummer.

We played several nights at the Morocco Room, but one of our more memorable gigs was at another club in LaCombe called The Honey Bee. Ernie decided to advertise the gig as "Ernie K-Doe's Anniversary." I asked him, "Anniversary of *what*?" He answered, "Anniversary of nothin', just an anniversary!" The Honey Bee was a double-wide trailer, located at the end of a gravel road. Out back was another trailer that was used as a whorehouse. Prostitutes lured drunken customers from the first trailer to the second. Being new to Louisiana, this was a little shocking to me. Obviously, the police knew what was happening but were not concerned.

K-Doe parked his pink 1959 Cadillac outside The Honey Bee. The car was equipped with long, silver trombone horns on each of the front fenders and an interior of white hair-like fluff. The back seat was reserved for Ernie's stage clothes, which hung from a golden rack. A photo of that car would have made a good album cover!

K-Doe's "Anniversary" began early in the afternoon, and by the time we started to play, most of the customers and our special guest artist, Benny Spellman, were drunk. Spellman, the low voice on "Mother-in-Law," lay sleeping on a pool table. As prostitutes tried to hustle men into their trailer, we began our set. In spite of all of this, the worst was yet to come. After the show, K-Doe told us the gig was a *benefit* and we weren't being paid. We were mad as hellhounds, packed up our instruments, and drove home.

Our next gig with K-Doe was at a much nicer club called Ruby's Roadhouse in nearby Mandeville, Louisiana. A large neon sign advertising Ernie K-Doe filled Ruby's beyond capacity. People stood in line at the door. My band began our set with a few instrumentals before calling K-Doe to the stage. As was his custom, Ernie opened the show with the hit "Mother-in-Law." K-Doe had recorded many regional hits, such as "A Certain Girl" and "I've Cried My Last Tear," but "Mother-in-Law" was his first (and only) national #1 hit record.

K-Doe was a great showman and performed James Brown-style dance steps and spins, tricks with the microphone, and even splits. When he did the splits at Ruby's, two funny things happened. Drunk on whiskey, he had trouble getting up from the floor. After he managed to crawl to his feet, he realized he had ripped the seat of his pants! This called for a quick change in wardrobe.

Overall, the show was a huge success. People paid twenty dollars at the door, and much money was collected. After the gig, K-Doe walked to the bandstand and paid us each a measly fifty dollars while he kept hundreds for himself. I had hired some of the best musicians in New Orleans, and they expected a lot more. It was time for a serious talk, something K-Doe didn't expect.

In Ruby's parking lot, I told Ernie to take a seat in my Chevy Blazer. I said, "Ernie, I respect you for being a star. I respect you for having hit records. But I've been working with stars all my life. You have to pay us decent wages. We're professionals and need at least $100 per night, or we won't play!" K-Doe's jaw dropped open in astonishment and his eyes widened like an owl searching for prey. He was used to working with kids who were eager to play with a star, no matter what he paid them. Realizing that I meant what I was saying, K-Doe shook my hand and agreed to pay us more in the future. Ironically our next gig would be a benefit, this time legitimate, and pay nothing. And yet, it proved to be a valuable "step up the ladder" for me in the New Orleans music scene.

Radio station WWOZ was presenting a benefit concert at an important club in the French Quarter called Storyville Jazz Hall. Many famous musicians had played Storyville, including Ray Charles and Fats Domino. This would be my first chance to play "The Quarters." All of our musicians agreed to play. Many famous artists were also playing the benefit, including Allen Toussaint, who wrote K-Doe's "Mother-in-Law" and many other hit records, including "Southern Nights" and "Working in the Coal Mine."

Storyville was a large show club, located on Decatur Street near the Old French Market. We edged our way through hundreds of people as we rolled my organ to the stage. Once the B3 was set up, I went to the bar for a beer. En route, a man approached me and said his name was King Floyd. I'd heard of Floyd because of his hit record "Groove Me, Baby" and politely shook his hand.

When Floyd became aware that I was the bandleader, he became arrogant and said, "I hope you know *all* of my songs!" I replied, "Do you have chord charts?" King Floyd answered, "No, you're supposed to know *all* my songs. My songs are classics!" I was getting angry and answered, "I didn't know we were working with you tonight. In fact, I've only heard *one* of your hits, 'Groove Me Baby.'

If you're a professional, you should have charts." At this statement, Floyd went into a rage. He told me that *he* would play organ. I have a laughable tape of King Floyd trying to play my Hammond.

After Floyd left the stage, I went back to the organ and decided to play my arrangement of "Basin Street Blues," which included a segue to the traditional New Orleans funeral march, "Closer Walk With Thee." While we were playing, I noticed a familiar face smiling at me from the dance floor. With bald head and white goatee, there stood world-famous jazz clarinetist, Pete Fountain! When we finished the set, Mr. Fountain enthusiastically shook my hand. I said, "It's an honor to meet you, sir!" To my amazement, Pete replied, "I'm honored to meet *you!*"

Pete Fountain insisted on buying me a drink. We walked to the bar and drank some Dixie beers together. When I asked him about his life and childhood, he said, "I know what you're getting at. All the kids hated me in high school, and I was a terrible student. Music was my only salvation!" Several months later, Anne and I were watching *The Tonight Show* with Johnny Carson. The special guest was Pete Fountain, and we heard him play *my* arrangement of "Basin Street" on national TV! I was surprised, yet honored. I also realized why Mr. Fountain had paid such close attention to my music.

I continued to work with Ernie K-Doe during the following year and began booking his gigs myself. It was the only way I could guarantee my band a decent income. At first, Ernie was satisfied with $300 per night for himself but soon upped his price to $500, the remainder going to the band. My musicians always made at least $100 per gig, sometimes more, and I paid myself the same as my band. I booked the K-Doe gigs for a guaranteed price, usually $1000 for two shows. This allowed me to pay K-Doe his $500 and my band $100 each. Then came the admission money that patrons paid at the door; *door money.* There were two ways I dealt with this: I'd either make a deal with the club owner that we'd play for $1,000 *or* "the door," whichever was higher. If we received extra money, I divided it equally with members of my band. Sometimes each musician was able to make $200 per night, which was top pay in the 1980s and even today.

Eventually K-Doe began raising his price above $500 per night, which prevented me from paying my musicians what they deserved.

I was no longer able to book gigs with Ernie, so he hired some Cajun kids who were overly impressed with his stardom and willing to work for "chump change." I took a six-month gig at a club called "Rhythms" on Bourbon Street with bluesman J. Monque'D and never saw Ernie again.

Ernie K-Doe and I parted as friends, and I will always have great respect and love for him. He was an outstanding singer, showman, and unique human being. Shortly before his death in 2001, I called Ernie at his now-famous Mother-in-Law Lounge in New Orleans to tell him I had been nominated for a Grammy with The Dukes of Dixieland. K-Doe's last words to me were, "You deserve it, Ricky. I'm proud of you!"

Chapter 27

Allen Toussaint, Sea-Saint Studios

When we first moved to Louisiana in 1983, I visited most of New Orleans' recording studios hoping for session work. This included the renowned Sea-Saint Studios, owned by famed songwriter and musician Allen Toussaint and producer Marshall Sehorn. I left my resume with Allen's son, Reggie, but didn't hear from Sea-Saint until nine years later. If I had played Reggie a few licks on the Hammond, I might have heard back sooner.

In 1992, I received a call from Roger Branch, chief engineer at Sea-Saint. Roger said I had been recommended by Carlo Ditta, owner of Orleans Records, and Luther Kent, a local blues singer who once sang with Blood, Sweat and Tears. Roger was working on a project for R. J. Reynolds Tobacco Company, an album called *Meet the Hard Packs*, available with saved-up Camel Cash coupons. I was happy to have the chance to do studio work, and took the Camel project seriously.

Despite the fact that I'd recorded for most major record labels in Los Angeles, I had only played one session in New Orleans. It was with

"Mighty" Sam McClain for Orleans Records and recorded in the basement of an old house. Sam's record was an "extended play" CD called *Your Perfect Companion*, and contained only four songs, two of which had already been recorded. Sam thought the first two songs weren't soulful enough and wanted to record two more, using Kerry Brown on drums, Billy Gregory on guitar, Richard Bird on bass, and me on Hammond organ. We managed to record two great songs in that hot basement, a blues called "Backstreets" and the Sam Cooke classic "A Change is Gonna Come." I helped with the arrangement on "A Change is Gonna Come," trying to breathe new life into the song. When the CD was released, my Hammond organ was a dominant instrument in the final mix. I used many glissandos in the appropriate places and Billy Gregory played some nice guitar licks reminiscent of Steve Cropper's great work with Otis Redding at Stax Records in Memphis.

The "Mighty Sam" session was nothing compared to a chance to work at Allen Toussaint's studio. Sea-Saint Studios was legendary, and had recorded many big name artists, including Etta James, Patti LaBelle, Dr. John, and even Paul McCartney. The walls of Sea-Saint were covered with gold and platinum records, Grammy nominations, and citations that Toussaint had won over his career. In the parking lot was Allen's gold Rolls Royce with a custom license plate that read "PIANO."

On my first day at the studio, Allen asked me to jam with him. An accomplished pianist, he began improvising a tune on the Steinway. I was at the Hammond and couldn't figure out which key he was playing in. It sounded like the key of *G*, but something was wrong. After a few minutes of searching, Allen yelled, "Key of G *flat*." I realized what Toussaint was doing: testing my musicianship by playing in a difficult key. Sometimes, jazz musicians like Coltrane used this method to evaluate musicians. I managed to survive the song in *G flat*, and then let loose on a jazz number in the key of *F*. Allen stopped playing piano and walked up to me with a smile on his face. I'd passed the test. He said, "I don't know if there's room in this town for both of us!" Of course, Allen meant this to be taken tongue-in-cheek. He was (and is) a master at piano, but he doesn't play organ, which requires a different style and technique.

Allen and I both played on the Camel cigarette project, but that would be our only session together. It had nothing to do with me personally. Allen had his own band with an organist named Sammy who played on his sessions. I was hired by Sea-Saint to work as house organist on all other projects that required organ and/or piano. My employers were Allen's business partner, Marshall Sehorn, who discovered Wilbert Harrison and produced the monster hit, "Kansas City," and chief engineer Roger Branch.

A few weeks after the Camel project, I was asked to overdub piano on an album by blues singer/guitarist Brint Anderson, titled *Homage to Elmore* (James), later released on Tomato Records. My job was to add blues piano to all seventeen songs, which took me two days to complete.

The album included many blues standards by Elmore like "Dust My Broom" and "The Sky is Crying." While I was overdubbing piano on "Dust My Blues," I saw Allen Toussaint in the control booth, listening to my playing and watching me through the glass window. I won't deny that I'm a pretty good blues pianist, but I never expected what Allen did next.

When I finished playing "Dust My Broom," I saw Toussaint standing in the control booth, clapping his hands. Allen led our engineer, assistant engineer, and secretary into the recording room where I was seated at the piano. They were clapping their hands and shouting, "Bravo!" This was something that just *doesn't happen* in a recording studio, especially when initiated by a musical genius like Allen Toussaint. It was one of the greatest honors of my life.

I learned a lot by listening to Allen's piano playing on the Camel sessions. Playing B3 was easy for me, but I wanted to learn "studio" piano that would be fitting for all popular music. Allen made it seem so easy and simple. He listened to the music and played chords and "tasty" fills at exactly the right places, usually between vocal lines or at the end of verses. He'd tell the other musicians, "Don't worry about me; I'll just be answering you." I came to understand his "statement and answer" piano strategy and am now able to record both organ and piano on important sessions.

Over a period of ten years, I played on many sessions at Sea-Saint, including an album by Robert Parker, (who recorded the hit "Barefootin' "), titled *An Introduction to Robert Parker*, and an album by Freddy Fender titled *Close to My Heart*, which would to be the last album he recorded before his death in 2006. I'll elaborate on those sessions in the following chapters.

Another Sea-Saint session worth mentioning was with singer and pianist extraordinaire Marcia Ball, who was asked to perform on a compilation CD of songs written by zydeco musician Boozoo Chavez. For those who aren't familiar with the term, "zydeco" is a form Cajun blues, usually performed by black artists. Zydeco music was originally created at house dances, where families and friends gathered for barbeque and beer.

This album, *Boozoo Hoodoo*, released by Fuel 2000 Records, Los Angeles, in 2007, involved many artists, each asked to contribute one song. Marcia Ball decided to record a Chavez original called "Dance the Night Away." This catchy yet simple song was easily recorded with Marcia on piano, myself on organ, and our rhythm section, which included Allyn Robinson on drums, Robert Wilson on bass, and Roger Branch on guitar. I'd been working with male and female musicians since I was fifteen, but had never heard a woman play R&B and blues piano as well as Marcia. On Hammond organ, I wouldn't be afraid to follow anybody on stage, but on piano I would never follow Marcia Ball. She'd rip me to shreds!

During this period of about ten years, I also played on many albums for Carlo Ditta's Orleans Records. I first met Carlo in 1984 when he came to hear our band with "Mighty" Sam McClain and Kerry Brown at the Teachers' Lounge in Gretna. Carlo was accompanied by a young guitar player named Billy Gregory. Carlo liked my organ playing and said that Billy had recently returned from California where he'd been playing with a band called "It's a Beautiful Day." I'd never heard of this band. The name sounded silly and miles away from my beloved down-home blues. My opinion was soon to change when Billy plugged his Les Paul into an amp and played some of the best slide guitar I'd ever heard. Despite the name of his former band, Billy Gregory was (and is) one of the most masterful guitar players I've ever heard.

This brings to mind the words of my musical mentor and tenor sax wizard, Tom Fabré. When I mentioned to Tom that I wanted to be the best organ player in Louisiana, he said, "Rick, nobody's the 'best.' When musicians reach a certain point of excellence, it's just a matter of style. Some people might like the style of Jimmy Smith better than 'Groove' Holmes, or the style of B.B. King better than Howlin' Wolf, but that doesn't mean that anyone is better than another. It's just a matter of opinion, and no great musician is *ever* the best! All you can hope for is to be *one* of the best!" Wise words that I try to remember.

My first session for Orleans Records was with "Mighty" Sam McClain, with Billy Gregory on guitar and Kerry Brown on drums, as mentioned in a previous chapter. During the following years, I played keyboards on eight more albums for Orleans Records, the most interesting with artists Coco Robicheaux and Rockie Charles. After Carlo Ditta built a studio in Covington, Louisiana, he called and asked me to do a session with "Coco." When I met Carlo at the studio, I asked if the session was with Koko Taylor. He replied, "No, it's with Coco Robicheaux." I'd never heard of Coco, but after I met him and heard him sing, he became a man I'd never forget.

Coco was a Cajun with a very raspy and soulful voice. He even drank shots of Tabasco sauce on stage to make his voice more hoarse. He wore a long braided pony tail that reached below his hips, as well as an array of voodoo charms around his neck and a black cowboy hat. He might well have been the strangest looking artist I'd ever encountered, but man, could Coco sing! Soul, soul, and more soul. Once I heard his music, I gained immediate respect for the man. His voice was so unique and emotional that he could have shared the stage with any R&B or rock singer. He sounded like Rod Stewart with soulful laryngitis. I played on two albums with Coco: *Spiritland*, recorded in 1994 for Orleans Records, and *Hoo Doo Party*, recorded in 2000 and released by Orleans Records and Sky Ranch Records, Paris. (Coco was very popular in France.)

To promote the *Spiritland* CD, Carlo booked Robicheaux to play the House of Blues in New Orleans, backed by his studio band, which included me on organ. Coco arrived at the gig wearing voodoo charms and his trademark three-foot ponytail. When we went on stage, he sat on a short stool and sang for a sold-out crowd. There was a king-size bottle of Tabasco sauce on the floor, which he'd grab between songs and shake into his mouth. The audience loved Coco at the House of Blues as he was loved by all who knew him in New Orleans. Sadly, Coco died from a heart attack in 2011 while standing outside a French Quarter nightclub. His life was celebrated with a New Orleans jazz funeral, but his music was never fully appreciated in other parts of America. Coco Robicheaux died a star in Louisiana and France but remains unknown in most parts of the U.S.A.

Another interesting session I played for Orleans Records was with tugboat captain Rockie Charles. Carlo Ditta had a knack for finding obscure, undiscovered artists and Rockie Charles was no exception. Rockie got ideas for melodies and lyrics while piloting his tugboat on the Mississippi River before going home to record them on cassettes, accompanying himself on guitar. Rockie had a soft and pretty voice, somewhat like Al Green, and his lyrics were tender and original, but there was just one problem: he had absolutely no idea of how to construct a song.

Carlo said that Rockie's rhythm tracks had already been recorded and asked me to overdub organ. I thought this R&B session would be quick and easy until I began listening to Rockie's songs in my earphones. The lyrics were soulful, the vocals were nice, but the music was as disjointed as a chicken trying to fly with a broken wing. The chord changes Rockie played on guitar flew in different directions with every verse and chorus. If a song was in the key of A Major, he might stay in that key for eight measures, ten measures, twelve measures, maybe sixteen and a half measures before going to the next chord of perhaps D Major, and God only knew how long he'd stay in D Major before the next chord change! To make matters worse, there was no way to know when he'd decide to switch from major chords to minor chords, *even in the middle of the same measure!* Even Rockie didn't know. He'd just change chords when he felt the urge. I had never played with a musician without any conception of song structure, and what I thought would be an easy session became one of my most tedious. No musician on earth could follow him without a crystal ball!

Having a "never give up" attitude, I decided the only way I could overdub organ on Rockie's album was in short segments. Producer Carlo Ditta brought me a remote control device that connected to his tape recorder. With this keypad, I was able to start, rewind, stop, and re-record at any point during a song while overdubbing organ. I didn't need Carlo's help for this patchwork method of recording, so he left me alone in the studio to "stitch" appropriate organ parts into Rockie's songs. I spent all day working on Rockie's album until my head was spinning, and Carlo was satisfied with my playing. This CD, titled *Born for You,* was released on Orleans Records in 1996.

In order to promote the album, Carlo booked Rockie and a small band with me on organ to perform at the all-important New Orleans Jazz and Heritage Festival. We'd be playing for a huge crowd, including people from the recording industry. After just one rehearsal, we found ourselves on stage in front of hundreds of excited potential fans. Before I took my seat at the Hammond B3 organ, I gathered our musicians together and said, "Don't try to follow Rockie. It's impossible. Just follow me! Watch for my signals and listen to my organ. Rockie will have to follow *us*!" This strategy worked, and after our performance Rockie Charles received much applause from the crowd. People from the recording industry swamped the stage, passing out their cards to Rockie and members of our band.

Despite its lack of musical form, one of my favorite songs is Rockie's "Old Black Joel." It's as soulful as anything I've heard from Otis Redding or Joe Tex. As was the case with Coco Robicheaux (and many talented artists), Rockie died in 2010 unknown to most of the world beyond Louisiana, even though he'd been touring Ontario, Canada, and was building a rather large following in Toronto. Just as Rockie was gaining popularity in Canada, he heard the haunting sound of a distant foghorn. His old tugboat was calling out, "It's time, Captain Rockie! Time to cross that big ol' river. We're goin' home."

Chapter 28
Ernie K-Doe's Funeral

When I die want you to bury me
In my high top Stetson hat
Put a $20 gold piece on my watch chain
And they'll know I died standin' pat

I want six crap shooters for pall bearers
And ten purtty women to sing my song
I want a jazz band to play "When the Saints go Marchin' In"
And raise hell as we stroll along.

St. James Infirmary Blues

There is no such thing as a happy funeral, but Ernie K-Doe's memorial at Gallier Hall came close. The self-proclaimed "Emperor of the Universe" was eulogized with joy and sent back to Heaven wearing a crown.

Gallier Hall is an imposing building on St. Charles Avenue in New Orleans. It's where many dignitaries have lain in state, including governors, senators, mayors, and even Jefferson Davis, President of the Confederate States of America. On Mardi Gras Day, the mayor of New Orleans is always situated on a large platform in front of Gallier Hall. From there, he gives a welcome toast to King Zulu, king of New Orleans' first black krewe, as the Zulu parade momentarily stops its march up St. Charles. Next, when the Krewe of Rex parade arrives, the mayor toasts Rex, "King of Carnival," and presents him with the symbolic key to the city. The mayor lifts his glass and proclaims, "Hail Rex! Hail Rex! Hail Rex!" as onlookers cheer, and the Rex parade resumes its journey up St. Charles Avenue and onto Canal Street. People come from all over the world to see this historic event. It was a great honor for Ernie K-Doe's funeral celebration to take place in Gallier Hall.

Anne and I entered a large room where Ernie lay in state. We were lucky to find two fold-up chairs, as the room would soon be filled to capacity with about 300 people. We loved the man, and it was sad to see his body in a coffin. He had slept at our home and was our friend. But in a strange way, we were happy for him. Dressed entirely in white, K-Doe was adorned with gold Mardi Gras beads and a beautiful crown of *faux* diamonds. There was nothing funny about the fake diamonds. In New Orleans, fantasy becomes reality. Ernie K-Doe had christened himself "Emperor of the Universe," and he looked the part.

Several musicians performed at K-Doe's funeral, but the most impressive was Allen Toussaint, who composed the song "Mother-in-Law" that made Ernie an international star. Toussaint sat at a black Steinway grand, and played a medley of K-Doe's tunes. His music was beautiful. Tears turned to happy smiles when he played one of K-Doe's up-beat songs, "Te-Ta-Te-Ta-Ta," a local favorite that probably never made it beyond the South but lifted the spirits of everyone at the "funeral" as they sang along. In New Orleans, funerals are more a celebration of a person's life than the mournful, almost macabre solemnity observed elsewhere. A "jazz funeral" is how most of us would like to be remembered by our loved ones. Dancing in the streets, not tears on our cheeks.

To avoid the bottleneck of well-wishers at the end of the ceremony, Anne and I decided to leave ahead of the crowd. We watched as TV cameras focused on the front of Gallier Hall, awaiting K-Doe's casket. It was a sad irony that many of these people didn't care much about Ernie while he lived. Club owners considered him a "crazy, undependable alcoholic" and were reluctant to hire him. When I was booking K-Doe, I'd tell the club owners that I could promise them at least one good show, which would pack the house and make them money. The second show was always questionable, depending upon how drunk K-Doe became. Ernie quit drinking shortly before his death, with the help of his wife, Antoinette.

There was something special about K-Doe that made people love him. Not only was he "Mr. Mother-in-Law," but also "Mr. Charisma." It was virtually impossible not to like the man, and I've never heard anyone say they hated Ernie. Comments about his faults are always accompanied with understanding laughs and smiles. "Oh, that's just K-Doe!" people still say.

As a brass band played "Just a Closer Walk With Thee," K-Doe's casket was carried to an elegant horse-drawn hearse, painted black with frosted windows. Atop the hearse sat a little black man wearing a stovepipe hat. In his hands were the reins to a team of white horses. The hearse, followed by hundreds of "second-liners" twirling colorful umbrellas, marched several miles to a crypt in the famous St. Louis cemetery where K-Doe's body would spend eternity. Thousands of people lined the streets to watch the procession. New Orleans mayor Marc Morial ordered many streets to be closed, from Interstate I-10 to St. Charles, from Poydras Street to Esplanade Avenue. Almost half of downtown New Orleans was closed to traffic in honor of Ernie K-Doe!

Ernie K-Doe lived his last years in self-anointed glory. He and his wife opened a little club called the Mother-In-Law Lounge in New Orleans. It became a tourist attraction, but like many great artists, K-Doe was never fully appreciated in his hometown until after his death. Charity Hospital in New Orleans was where poor kids were born and poor people died. Ernie K-Doe did both, and was laid to rest in a donated tomb. During his sixty-five years of life, he made millions of people happy with his music, yet he died without enough money to pay for his own burial.

Ernie K-Doe embodied the magic of New Orleans. If you were to visit St. Louis Cemetery and see K-Doe's name inscribed on a slab of stone, you might imagine him shouting, "Hey, get out of this place! I'm not here, fool. Take a walk through the French Quarter and you'll see me clowning in every bar, singing with every band, and dancing in the streets!"

Chapter 29

Grammy Nomination

The Dukes Of Dixieland
with The Moses Hogan Gospel Choir

Driving home from work on a winter day in the year 2000, Anne was listening to the car radio. As she waited for a train to finish crossing Highway 190 in Slidell, she heard some news that would give credence to my life as a recording musician.

"You've been nominated for a Grammy!" screamed my wife as she rushed into our house. I couldn't believe it, and checked the Grammy site on my computer. Sure enough, an album I'd recorded with The Dukes of Dixieland had been nominated for a Grammy! After forty years in music, recording hundreds of songs and never striking gold, I had finally received the highest honor in the music business. It may be a cliché for performers to say that being nominated is all that matters and they don't care if they win, but in my case, this was true. I didn't care about winning the contest. I was thrilled and happy to be part of a Grammy nomination, and to receive a certificate from the National Academy of Recording Arts and Sciences.

From that day forth, the words "Grammy Nominated Organist" would precede my name. I could use the Grammy insignia on my letterhead and business cards. Thoughts of my eventual obituary crossed my mind. Memories of my parents' disdain for my music brought a strange feeling of satisfaction. Pride is a terrible thing, but my heart was filled with justification. Justification of my crazy life and my refusal to ever quit playing. I was a very happy man on January 4, 2000.

There is an odd twist of fate involved with The Dukes of Dixieland. When I was in the eighth grade in Whittier, one of my friends was Ronnie Bernard. He was from New Orleans and his brother, (or half-brother), played bass with the Dukes in the 1950s. In Ronnie's bedroom closet was one of the jackets his brother wore on stage. Ronnie said it was called a "one-button roll," which meant the white silk lapels went straight down without indentations until they reached a button at waist's length. I thought it was the coolest coat I'd ever seen. I was thirteen years old, and remember trying on that jacket and looking at myself in a mirror. How I dreamed of being a musician, like Ronnie's brother.

Over the years, The Dukes of Dixieland went through many personnel changes. Musicians died, others retired. In the 1990s, I was surprised to learn that the Dukes' current bandleader, Richard Taylor, lived in our little town of Bayou Lacombe. An excellent drummer, Richard and his wife Bobbi lived only a few miles from our home. We became friends and recorded several albums together at Sea-Saint Studios. Another coincidence was that my first road-gig was at the Top Hat Lounge in Kankakee, Illinois, in 1961 when I was eighteen. Richard Taylor played the same club in that same year.

Richard liked my playing, and offered me a piano job with the Dukes. I knew I wasn't proficient enough on jazz piano to cut the gig and declined the offer. Later, destiny entered the picture when Richard and the Dukes decided to record a gospel/jazz album that required an organist. Richard hired me for the session, and I was paid $500 to record five songs.

Recording a gospel album was a brilliant idea for the Dukes. It combined, perhaps for the first time in history, a black gospel choir with Dixieland jazz. The New Orleans Gospel Choir, led by the late piano and vocal virtuoso Moses Hogan, was spine tingling, powerful, and profound. When we cut the album at Ultrasonic Studios in New

Orleans, I was somewhat in awe of Moses Hogan and the Dukes. I'd never played Dixieland jazz, but was familiar with black gospel music from listening to artists like James Cleveland and Sister Bessie Griffin. As things turned out, I had nothing to fear. All I had to do was play the correct chord changes on organ with a gospel/blues feeling, and let the Dukes play their Dixieland horn parts. This was easier than I had expected, and my employers were happy with my playing.

The album was unique enough to draw critical acclaim. I sensed something very special about the project and commented to the producer, "I think this is Grammy material." My intuition proved true. The album *Gloryland* was released by Leisure Jazz Records in Hollywood and deservedly nominated by the Recording Academy as "Best Contemporary Gospel Album of 1999." It's one of the best albums I've ever recorded.

When my Grammy certificate arrived, I took it to a photographer and had three copies made. One for our son Craig, another for daughter Kelli, and one for Marian Howard, my childhood piano teacher. Marian was in her nineties, but had always believed in my music. She sent me a wonderful letter in which she said that she was not only proud of me, but not the least bit surprised that I'd attained such an honor. She said that of all her students, spanning over forty years of teaching, I was the only one who was "gifted" enough to go professional. I couldn't share my happiness with my parents or grandparents because they were no longer living, but sharing the news with my childhood piano teacher was like getting a big gold star on this page of my life in music.

Some people mistakenly think that a Grammy Nomination wins money, while others believe it will provide the recipient with higher-paying gigs. Neither is the case. You can't go around telling other musicians you've been nominated for a Grammy. It would come across as egotistical bragging. The most I've done is to have the Grammy insignia printed on my business cards, which I can pass to other people without comment. A Grammy nomination isn't a "money thing"; it's the highest honor a musician can receive from his peers. It's something special, something that will make your children and grandchildren take note and be proud.

Chapter 30

Robert "Barefootin'" Parker
Oliver "Who Shot The Lala" Morgan

When Sea-Saint Studios producer Roger Branch called me for a session with Robert Parker, I couldn't place the name. Roger quickly reminded me that Parker had written and recorded the song "Barefootin' " in 1966. "Barefootin' " was a huge hit record, selling over a million copies and was played on radio stations in the U.S., Canada, and the United Kingdom. It was covered by Johnny Winter, Wilson Pickett, Alabama, and Pete Townshend. Parker's original version of "Barefootin' " is still being played on oldies radio today. My work with him would prove to be satisfying and fun, as well as frustrating.

When I met Robert Parker at the studio, he was dressed in a tailored (and obviously expensive) gray suit, white dress shirt, and tie. He looked and acted very much "the gentleman." Youthful in appearance, he claimed to be sixty years old. However, his musical history betrayed him. After checking his credentials on the Internet, I learned that Mr. Parker was actually seventy. He may have felt that people would think seventy was too old to make a comeback in music, or like many of us over forty, just decided to take ten years off his age. He looked young enough to easily pass for sixty or even fifty.

Not only was Robert Parker a singer, but he also played tenor sax. He was a studio musician in the late 1950s and early '60s, and played on many of the songs I loved as a teenager like "High Blood Pressure" by Huey "Piano" Smith and "Sick and Tired" by Chris Kenner. Parker also recorded with Lloyd Price, Larry Williams, Little Richard, Ray Charles, and Fats Domino.

In an effort to regain the spotlight, Parker cut more records over the ensuing years, and although none of them received much notice, when he heard our studio band he seemed enthusiastic. We'd all been "around the block" a few times and were able to communicate on a friendly, musically understandable basis with Parker. Our studio band consisted of old blues cats who were familiar with his New Orleans style of R&B. Also, he was happy that two of us had received Grammy nominations. Parker said, "That's just what I want. Grammy musicians!"

Our album with Parker included sixteen songs, two of which I'd written many years earlier. One was "The Way She Do It," a song I wrote in 1968. I was happy with Parker's version until I went to the studio to hear the final mix. While tapping my foot to the infectious Motown-style beat, I was shocked and jolted out of my seat when I heard a loud, female voice shouting over the choruses. I was dismayed. The girl's voice, which had been added when I wasn't at the studio, had destroyed my song. Her yelling voice was completely unnecessary and artistically terrible. After so many years of waiting for the song to be recorded, it had been ruined behind my back. All I could think of was, "Look what they've done to my song, Ma." This was very painful for me.

The second of my songs that Parker recorded was "Good Woman," a guilt-ridden love song I wrote for my wife during our troubled years in the late 1960s. After we recorded "Good Woman" and were listening to a playback in the control booth, I noticed that Robert Parker had tears in his eyes. He looked at me and said, "Those lyrics touch my heart. They're beautiful." It was nice to know that an accomplished artist appreciated my song. This album, *An Introduction to Robert Parker*, was released in 2006 by Fuel 2000 Records in Los Angeles. I was given no writers' credits for my songs and have never received any royalties. I mentioned this to co-producer Roger Branch and was told that none of the writers received credits on the CD from the record company. I'd been paid $1,000 for the Parker session and tried to forget the issue.

Before the album was released, Sea-Saint Studios wanted to give Parker some current exposure in New Orleans. I was playing the role of bandleader and assembled a powerhouse group of musicians to back him: bass, drums, guitar, and organ, augmented by a horn section of trumpet, baritone, and tenor saxophones. We put together a tight show in rehearsals, and I called nightclubs for bookings. I was in for a surprise.

In spite of the fact that Parker had sold millions of records with "Barefootin'," major club owners weren't interested in booking him. They didn't think Parker's name had enough drawing power. The House of Blues manager refused to return my phone calls, and the manager of Tipitina's, a legendary nightclub, said we could work "for the door" on a weeknight with no guaranteed salary. He said we couldn't have a weekend night because Robert Parker wasn't 'big enough' for a Friday, Saturday, or Sunday." It didn't matter that he'd sold millions of records; he just wasn't a "big enough attraction." Weeknight slots at Tipitina's for "the door" were for new bands, trying to build names for themselves. This cost the club nothing, essentially providing entertainment for free. I had a band of professional musicians and a "star" artist. I politely declined this insulting offer.

Because of our relationship with Allen Toussaint and Sea-Saint Studios, we were able to book the New Orleans Jazz and Heritage Festival, locally known as "Jazz Fest." Our show was to star both Robert Parker and a popular local singer, Oliver "Who Shot the LaLa" Morgan. After two rehearsals, we hit the stage at Jazz Fest with flying colors. Thousands of people watched our show and a TV crew filmed the entire performance.

Oliver Morgan opened the show with his local hit, "Who Shot the LaLa," a New Orleans R&B classic. Morgan was a happy showman. With a colorful umbrella in hand, he left the stage and led the crowd in a second-line parade in front of the bandstand while our band kept playing the "LaLa" song. After Morgan's show, Robert Parker came on stage and sang his hit, "Barefootin'." People in the audience kicked off their shoes and danced in the mud. Local newspaper and magazine reviews were excellent, but we were never asked to play Jazz Fest again. This was due to some "confusion" with the television company that filmed our show.

When I learned that *TRIO Network* of Canada (later *NBC Universal*), planned to broadcast our performance worldwide via satellite, I became suspicious. When I learned they had paid Robert Parker and Oliver Morgan $500 each for the television rights, I got angry. I had been in the music business too long to be ripped off. I didn't give a damn about the glory of being on TV. I wanted our band to be paid.

I phoned the manager of the TV company and told him I knew the laws concerning payment for televised music and images. I didn't threaten a lawsuit, but the threat was certainly implied. The producer was ambivalent and dismissive until I said I worked at Allen Toussaint's studio. This revelation caused him to take me seriously, and he asked me how much money I wanted. I said, "Two hundred dollars for each musician in my band," which amounted to $1,800. This gave him room to bargain, and I agreed to accept $1,000, which I divided equally with the band.

The next problem came from Robert Parker himself. After the death of Ernie K-Doe, his friends were asked to play a benefit for his widow, Antoinette. It was to be held at the Rock 'n' Bowl, a local bowling alley that had two bandstands for live music. Located in a shopping center in mid-city New Orleans, the Rock 'n' Bowl was situated on the second story, up a long and painful flight of stairs. Painful indeed for musicians carrying heavy equipment. In the middle of the stairway was an old iron banister. Musicians had to balance their amps, keyboards, and drums on this banister and slowly push them up the staircase, step by step.

The Rock 'n' Bowl is infamous for making Mick Jagger and Keith Richards pay admission to see a local band. It's probably the only nightclub in the world that would insult The Rolling Stones. Mick and Keith paid five dollars each, got their hands stamped with blue ink, and climbed the stairs. This was the mentality I had to deal with when we played the benefit for K-Doe's widow.

The owner of the Rock 'n' Bowl agreed to pay our musicians $100 each (including Robert Parker) while all the other acts performed *pro bono*. There was one condition: we were to leave our equipment on stage for the other bands to use. K-Doe had many friends, and stars like Allen Toussaint and King Floyd came to perform. A group called The Blue Eyed Soul Revue played the first set, using our instruments, before we went onstage to play a forty-five minute show with King Floyd. After a fifteen-minute break, Allen Toussaint took a seat at my Kurzweil piano and played some of K-Doe's hits, most of which he'd written. The Rock 'n' Bowl was completely packed with customers buying drinks, but our band's star, Robert Parker, was nowhere to be found.

I had a feeling that the club owner would use Parker's absence as an excuse not to pay us. He continued to ask me, "Where's Robert Parker?" His club was packed, his stage filled with famous musicians, but he still wanted Parker! I sensed this was a ploy. I was disappointed that Parker hadn't shown up for the gig, but his presence wouldn't have made any difference. The Rock 'n' Bowl was making piles of money selling drinks and food to our crowd. My only worry was not being able to pay my band. I decided to confront the "boss" while we still had a crowd of people and before we played our last set.

When the club owner asked me again about Robert Parker's absence, I answered with the question: "What will you do if Parker *never* gets here?" I was prepared to pull our amps, drums, guitars, and piano off the stage and stop the show, thereby losing his paying customers. Although unspoken, he was fully aware of this. He said, "If Parker doesn't show, then I'll cut his $100 from your pay, but you better be on that stage until *exactly* 2:00 a.m." He was on a power trip, but at least I'd made him promise to pay my band.

I called Parker's house on a cell phone and woke him from a peaceful sleep. He said he'd been stricken with diarrhea on his way to the gig, turned his car around, and gone home. I didn't believe his excuse for a minute because Parker never bothered to call the club. When I told the club owner that Robert Parker was sick, he repeated his demand, "You better damn well be on that stage until exactly 2:00 a.m." I don't like being "bossed" by anybody, let alone by the owner of a cheap bowling alley, but I had to "eat crow." I had my band to consider. Despite all my flaws, I always try to keep my word. I had promised my musicians $100 each for this gig, and I'd have borrowed their money from an ATM, if necessary.

With the help of local bluesman J. Monque'D and the great sax player Jerry Jumonville, we played the last set and rocked the house until closing time. Monque'D is a great showman and Jerry Jumonville has played sax with artists that almost stretch the imagination, from the Doobie Brothers to Bonnie Raitt, Smokey Robinson to Bette Midler.

With a show like ours plus the other artists who performed that night, the audience didn't have time to miss Robert Parker. Most of them had probably forgotten his name was on the billing. Parker's no-show was just a cheap excuse for the owner to rip off our band.

When I went to collect our money, the owner told me to meet him in an after-hours club located downstairs, where I waited like a humble sheep as he danced with his girlfriend. From time to time, he glanced in my direction, but kept dancing, song after song. He expected me to beg or go home, but after almost an hour he managed to walk my way. With a look of almost obscene authority, he gave me the money to pay my band. I needn't elaborate further about what I feel for this man: just ask Mick Jagger or Keith Richards!

Robert Parker and his wife live in the small town of Amite, Louisiana, about seventy miles north of New Orleans. The last news I've heard, Parker was working for the city, driving a yellow school bus. As a Roman slave once whispered in the ear of a victorious king, "All glory is fleeting!"

Chapter 31

Freddy Fender

Freddy Fender is a funny name, obviously contrived, and tends to create the misconception that the man might be taken lightly. Lightly, that is, until you were able to meet Freddy (Baldemar Huerta) face to face! A tall, imposing man with gray hair and nice features, he immediately commanded respect. He was a man who had gone from abject poverty in a small Mexican-American village in south Texas to the top of the recording industry, with hits "Before the Next Teardrop Falls" and "Wasted Days and Wasted Nights," both recorded in 1974. Freddy had also won three Grammy awards and had a star dedicated in his honor on Hollywood's Walk of Fame. He might have assumed a funny name, but there was nothing funny about the man. He was a serious and extremely talented musician.

In 2004, I got a call from Roger Branch at Sea-Saint Studios asking if I'd like to record a new album with Freddy. It would be a paid session, and I was glad to accept. We began to cut the tracks for what would be Freddy's last album before he died of cancer in 2006.

The CD was released on Fuel 2000 Records in 2004, titled *Freddy Fender, Close To My Heart.*

Freddy sat on a stool next to my piano, played guitar, and cut all his vocals live. If we made it through a song without obvious mistakes, that was a "take" so far as Freddy was concerned. This became frustrating for producer/engineer Roger Branch. A producer tries to make every song the best it can be, and usually asks for several cuts of each tune. From these cuts, the artist and producer usually decide upon the best version. Freddy would have nothing to do with this philosophy. If the first "take" sounded good to him, it was "in the can." We were all professional recording musicians and seldom made mistakes.

Roger wasn't happy with this attitude, but it didn't bother the other studio musicians. We were happy to move quickly through the album. Recording twenty-four songs in two days is hard to accomplish. In fact, we recorded twenty songs the first day, only four the next. As with most sessions, there were no rehearsals. Freddy would sing a song, strum the changes on guitar, and we'd listen and learn, right in the studio. If some of the chord changes were confusing, we'd write them down on manuscript paper.

During a coffee break, I asked Freddy if he'd like to record some songs in Spanish. I'd grown up near Los Angeles with its large Mexican population and loved the beauty of Mexican music, which was easily found on the radio. Freddy glanced at the floor in thought, then raised his head with a smile. "Yes," he said, "I'd like to do a song called "Que" (meaning *What* in English), and another song called "La Paloma" (*The Dove*). One of our musicians said, "Do you mean 'La Paloma Blanca'?" Freddy got a scowl on his face and said, "No, I *hate* that song! It has no feeling! There's another song called 'La Paloma' that I want to record."

When we returned to the studio, Freddy taught us the song "Que." It wasn't difficult, just three chords, although we had to remember when to make the changes. This wasn't hard if we listened to Freddy's singing, as it made the chord changes predictable. The ending went to a very "tasty" C major to F minor and back to C major. This was a nice ending and something I didn't expect. "La Paloma" was also a beautiful song that was easy to record, with only two chord changes. Again, our job was to determine where the changes came by listening to Freddy's voice.

Long before we recorded "Que" and "La Paloma," I'd realized that Freddy was an exceptionally good vocalist, but when I heard him singing in Spanish, he moved from "good" to "great." This didn't apply to my ears alone; the other musicians couldn't help but be impressed. Although they couldn't understand a word of Spanish, the language was far more beautiful than Germanic-rooted English. Whether English-speaking people want to admit it or not, Germanic languages are harsh and poetically cold, whereas Latin languages are much warmer, more musical, and more pleasing to the ear. This is why the greatest operas are performed in Italian. Freddy Fender's first language was Spanish, and when he sang in his parents' native tongue, he was able to touch the soulful roots of his childhood. His beautiful voice brought tears to my eyes and sent chills down my spine as every hair on my arms stood at full attention, like soldiers before a king. Funny name or not, Freddy Fender's voice was musical royalty. The world lost a great artist when Freddy died at the age of seventy.

Chapter 32

Hurricane Katrina

We knew that Katrina was coming. Everyone knew. It was all over the news. A category five hurricane headed straight for the New Orleans area. We saw images of this massive storm on television, so large that it almost covered the entire Gulf of Mexico. A truly ominous sight.

Many people decided to evacuate from New Orleans, but as history has sadly shown, not enough people left. Much of New Orleans is below sea level, which makes the city easily susceptible to flooding. There are many pumping stations to deal with this problem, but not enough for the torrential rains from Katrina combined with broken levees.

New Orleans is located on the *south* shore of Lake Pontchartrain. Anne and I live on the *north* shore of the lake in St. Tammany Parish, which is above sea level. Usually the only danger from water comes to those who live in close proximity to the lake or in poorly designed sub-divisions in low-lying areas. Our home is located five miles north of Lake Pontchartrain on a gradual uphill slope, which is a long way for water to be "pushed" by a storm. In fact, our area is listed by insurance carriers as "least likely to flood." For most of us living in St. Tammany Parish, the danger from hurricanes comes from high velocity winds and the mini-tornadoes they spawn, not from water, which is the main cause of death and devastation. There was nothing remarkable about our decision to stay home and ride out the storm. Many of our neighbors chose to do the same. They'd been through hurricanes before, and although they realized that Katrina was bigger and more threatening than storms they'd experienced in the past, most residents of our small town of Lacombe decided not to evacuate. There were other reasons for our decision to stay home.

Anne and I aren't prone to panic and didn't want to join the snail-paced mass of crawling cars on the Interstate filled with people from New Orleans searching for hotels and motels in Mississippi, Alabama, Texas, Georgia, Tennessee, and even Illinois. We also had our tabby cat Ratcliffe and our black Labrador Mercy to consider. They were our dear friends, like our own children, and we couldn't abandon them.

We also had to protect the contents of our home, which included my musical instruments, computer equipment, and irreplaceable mementos. New Orleans was under martial law, patrolled by the Louisiana National Guard, but our area had no law enforcement after we were ordered to evacuate. After the storm, it was up to every resident to protect his own property from looters and thieves that were running rampant throughout south Louisiana. Some residents posted large hand-drawn signs in front of their homes which read, "Enter and be shot!" Our house is secluded by trees and hedges and would be easily burglarized. We were on our own, like the days of the Old West, and kept a 12 gauge shotgun and .32 revolver close at hand.

Anne and I had tried our best to prepare for the storm. We bought a generator at Home Depot, two five-gallon cans of gasoline, flashlight batteries, canned ravioli, and several gallons of water. Our biggest mistake, other than not buying enough gasoline, was not withdrawing cash from our bank. We thought that credit cards would let us buy gas and other necessities once businesses reopened, but we were sadly mistaken. We had expected to be without electricity for a few days, but never imagined it would last for over two weeks. Without electricity to run business computers, credit cards were useless and signs saying "Cash Only" were taped to gas pumps and store windows.

On the evening before the hurricane, the sky had an eerie amber glow that foretold something momentous was about to occur. We'd experienced this in California, where the phenomenon is called "earthquake weather." Anne and I had survived California wildfires and earthquakes, as well as several Louisiana hurricanes, and weren't in fear for our lives. Nervous, tense, alert, and excited, but not afraid. To us, Katrina was almost like a movie, where reality becomes abstract.

When the storm hit, we were lucky to receive winds from the west "eye" of the hurricane, which blow from north to south, thereby attacking the north side of our house which is solid brick. No windows to be smashed and shattered, just a protective barrier. When you experience a storm like Katrina, it's difficult to remember the details, just as it's difficult to remember the details of a dream. You're running on adrenaline, coping with the situation minute by minute, second by second. Your brain doesn't have time to commit the events to memory, but I still remember the howling winds, the rain, the lightning and thunder, and the sound of trees breaking while others were uprooted and thundered to the ground. When gigantic, hundred-foot pines hit the earth near our house, we felt the vibration of their impact through our floor. Outside our window, other pine trees could be seen, bending like blades of grass. Tree limbs hit our roof almost constantly. Soon the roof began to leak and water poured from the ceiling fan in our master bedroom. Anne and I formed a bucket brigade to catch the water and pour it down the kitchen sink until I was able to cover our bed with a tarp.

For several weeks after the storm, it was difficult to walk in our yard. Fallen trees were everywhere. Thick pine branches were embedded in our roof and stood like cruel Christmas trees. Snakes slithered in the debris, and we saw one on the roof of our home. Our fuse box had been blown from the back of the house, but that made little difference. Telephone poles lay split and broken in the street, and we had no electricity or telephone service for many weeks. Not even cell phones worked because their relay towers had been blown asunder. When our generator ran out of gas, we were completely without power. We live in the country and our water comes from a well with an electric pump. Without water, we couldn't flush the toilets, wash dishes, or bathe. This made us realize the first essential of any home is water! Everything else is a secondary luxury.

For several days after the storm, it was impossible to buy gasoline for the generator. The stations couldn't pump gas without electricity. Eventually some gas stations managed to operate but wouldn't accept checks or credit cards, only cash. We had no cash on hand. Without a generator to power our fans, the heat in our house was almost suffocating. It was close to 100 degrees, day and night, without a wisp of breeze. It was like living under a dome of steaming heat.

Many people were concerned about our safety during and after Katrina. Unable to reach us by telephone, cell phone, email, or regular mail, our son Craig in California entered our names in an Internet "Missing Persons" list. Although we weren't "missing," this gave people the impression that we might not have survived the storm. All they were able to see were pictures of people stranded on rooftops and dead bodies floating in the flooded streets of New Orleans.

The main street (and only business area) of our town is Louisiana Highway 190, and electricity was restored there before it was restored to private homes. Gas stations were able to function and accept credit cards, our lone market was open for business, and even our small library opened its doors. The library had computer access and I took advantage of this to reach our email server, where I found letters from relatives, friends, and musicians who'd been unable to contact us. Emails came from all corners of the globe. England, Germany, Holland, Sweden, Canada, the U.S.A, and even Japan. I composed a form letter that I sent to all of these people, letting them know that we were alive and well, and thanking them for their concern. Next, I emailed my webmaster and asked him to post "Rick and Anne survived Katrina without injury" on my website's home page.

Somehow our "missing persons" status was posted on a website called Hollywood Hangover, which focuses on musicians who were playing the Sunset Strip in the 1960s and 1970s. Many musicians I'd never met sent emails or made entries in my website guestbook. Among these were Jimmy Greenspoon, keyboardist with Three Dog Night, and Chicago blues legend Otis Rush, whose music has been an inspiration for many musicians, including Stevie Ray Vaughn and myself. Otis was aware that I'd played with his friends Howlin' Wolf and Sonny Boy Williamson. After our telephone service was restored, we received a call from Otis and his wife, inviting us to stay with them at their Chicago apartment if our house was unlivable. They even offered to send us money, which we politely declined.

I assured them that we were OK but we deeply appreciated their offer.

Delaney Bramlett could hardly believe that I'd spoken with blues icon Otis Rush, who had recently suffered a stroke. Because of the stroke, Otis had difficulty speaking and his wife had to translate his words for me. But Otis could still sing! I told him I loved his music and sang the first line of one of his songs, *"All the love I miss lovin',"* to which Otis sang the second line, *"All the kiss I miss kissin'."* Then we both laughed. After we regained postal service, Otis and his wife sent us a package of his DVDs, photos, and a signed greeting card that we framed for my music room. Jimmy Greenspoon also sent us a package, containing the latest Three Dog Night CD and his very interesting autobiography, *One is the Loneliest Number*. These acts of kindness show that there's a real bond between musicians, even if they've never met.

On a personal level, Katrina destroyed Sea-Saint Studios with flood waters. The beautiful Steinway piano, the pristine Hammond B3, and most of the electronic equipment were ruined beyond repair. Sea-Saint Studios was lost forever and is now a hair salon. When Sea-Saint was destroyed by Katrina, my job as studio keyboardist also fell victim to the storm. Because of Allen Toussaint's reputation, Sea-Saint was able to attract recording artists from all over America and Europe with the financial backing to hire local musicians for their sessions, in hopes of getting the "New Orleans Sound." Without Sea-Saint, the other studios in New Orleans usually record local bands with their own musicians.

I've only played a handful of sessions since Katrina, some with former Sea-Saint engineer Roger Branch at his Oak Street Studios and others for Carlo Ditta of Orleans Records. Although I recently played the French Quarter Festival, I refuse to play clubs for "chump change." During my many years in music, I've suffered too much, learned too much, and become proficient enough to never again sell my soul for less money than bartenders and waitresses. I started at the bottom (more than once) and inched my way up the slippery ladder of the music business. There is a saying in Taoist philosophy that one should know "when to stop!" I almost reached the top of that slippery ladder, and I've no intention of sliding back down. Except for sessions and meaningful gigs, it's time for me to take the Taoist advice. Katrina may have slammed the door on my career as a studio musician, but it opened another that has given me the opportunity to write this book.

Epilogue

El Monte Legion Stadium, where I met Ritchie Valens in 1958, was demolished in 1974. It was my childhood dream to play there, and although that never happened, other dreams took its place. From tiny nightclubs to vast concert halls, I've played for many thousands of people. I was only a sideman, but was able to fulfill whatever destiny had in store. I never cared about getting rich from music, but I did see myself playing professionally. The wealth in my life has come in many other ways.

Sometimes I wonder why I was born with musical talent. Was it inherited, or was there a purpose? I once asked Muddy Waters this question: "What would happen if all music were to stop?" His answer, "The world would go mad!" This made me realize that music and other forms of art are necessary ingredients in the great scheme of things. If my music made people happy and helped them forget their troubles, then I suppose my life has been worthwhile. But in all honesty, I'm no musical humanitarian. I play music because I love music, and if my audience loves it too, so much the better.

If I could go back in time and talk to the young man I was at El Monte Legion Stadium in 1958, I might say to him, "Boy, if you really want to be a musician you must dedicate yourself completely to that goal. Music has to come first, above all else. A few years in garage bands will not suffice. You need to devote your life to music, over the wishes of your parents, your future wife, and anyone else. You must be willing to go to bed with an empty stomach, play for free, and be prepared to suffer *anything* in order to play your songs.

"It's not enough to have talent. Many musicians and singers who are as good as, if not better than, big-name stars have to play trashy clubs for chump change. There's also an element of luck involved in the music business. You have to be in the right place at the right time to be discovered by talent scouts and record company executives or have an opportunity to play with famous musicians who can help your career. These lucky moments might never happen, but that's the chance you take. Your desire to be a musician is a *calling*, no less than that of a minister. There's no financial security in music, and some musicians trade their talent for a steady job. But if you give up your dreams for money, you'll be selling your very soul.

I've lived my life for music, and wouldn't hesitate to do it again. It's been an exciting, happy adventure. Fun, unpredictable, crazy, and free. But most important of all, my life in music brought me a wonderful wife, whose words "I married a musician" carried me through times of trouble and despair. Without her, my life would have been empty.

Afterword

When I was a young boy
I wasn't too good lookin'
And one thing that is certain
I wasn't too strong

Got kicked out of high school
'Cause I'd just sit there thinkin'
Starin' out the window
And hummin' a song

I couldn't even fight good
It was back in the 50s
My friends were only outcasts
My feet were too long

I never could play football
But I could play piano
And I knew playin' music
Was where I belonged

As I became a young man
My folks were disappointed
They wanted me to someday be
A big businessman

My mother used to tell me
Have fun with your music
But never let it interfere
With serious plans

So I left home one mornin'
I left my folks a letter
Said I'd be headin' Eastward
To play in a band

Maybe I'll get famous
Or I might just die a poor man
But I'll be playing music
And I don't give a damn!

(From the song "This Life I Give To Music" by Rick Allen, Copyright 1975)

Rick Allen Discography

Year	Album	Artist	Credit
1964	Fanny Mae	Sonny Boy Williamson	Keyboards
1964	Farmer John	The Skunks	Keyboards
1964	Justine	The Skunks	Keyboards
1966	I Still Need You	Bobby Angelle	Keyboards
1968	Black & the White of It Is the Blues	Joanne Vent	Keyboards
1968	I Used To Be Happy	Bobby Angelle	Keyboards
1968	No Other Love	Bobby Angelle	Keyboards
1968	Too Much For You	Bobby Angelle	Keyboards
1973	They Love Me They Love Me Not	Genya Ravan	Keyboards

Year	Album	Artist	Credit
1974	Don Preston	Don Preston	Keyboards
1975	Giving Birth to a Song	Delaney Bramlett	Keyboards
1975	It's Really Love	Delaney Bramlett	Keyboards
1976	Nothing Without You	Delaney Bramlett	Keyboards
1977	Class Reunion	Delaney Bramlett and Friends	Keyboards
1978	Delaney Bramlett w/Steve Cropper	Delaney Bramlett w/Steve Cropper	Keyboards
1992	Meet the Hardpacks	The Hardpacks	Organ, Keyboards
1995	Homage to Elmore	Brint Anderson Band	Keyboards
1995	Live at Grand Casino	The Boogie Kings	Hammond B3
1995	Modern Blues Anthology: Ain't Times Hard	Various Artists	Performer
1995	Spiritland	Coco Robicheaux	Keyboards
1995	Your Perfect Companion	Mighty Sam McClain	Keyboards

Year	Album	Artist	Credit
1996	Born For You	Rockie Charles	Organ, Piano, Keyboards
1996	Swamp Boogie	Little Freddy King	Organ, Keyboards, Wurlitzer
1999	Blues Shakers	Various Artists	Performer
1999	Gloryland	The Dukes of Dixieland	Keyboards
1999	Orleans Record Story	Various Artists	Organ, Keyboards, Piano (Electric)
2000	King	Rick Allen	Keyboards, Organ (Hammond)
2000	Hoo Doo Party	Coco Robicheaux	Organ, Piano, Keyboards
2000	Sounds From Home	Delaney Bramlett	Organ, Organ (Hammond)
2001	Hawaiian Sounds	Buster Walea	Piano, Organ (Hammond)
2001	New Orleans Sessions	Freddy Fender	Piano, Organ (Hammond)
2001	Robert Parker	Robert Parker	Piano, Organ (Hammond)
2002	Back In Time	Willie Tee	Piano

Year	Album	Artist	Credit
2002	Soul of Money Records	Various Artists	Piano, Celeste
2003	Boozoo Hoodoo!: The Songs of Boozoo Chavis	Various Artists	Organ (Hammond)
2003	This Is Love	Josephine Mills	Piano
2004	Close to My Heart	Freddy Fender	Piano, Organ (Hammond)
2006	Legendary Performers	Mickey Gilley/ Freddy Fender	Piano & Organ
2007	Classics	Freddy Fender	Piano & Organ
2007	Soul of Money Records Volume 2	Various Artists	Celeste
2007	Introduction to Robert Parker	Robert Parker	Piano & Organ
2008	Ace 30th Birthday Celebration: Soul & Funk CD Import	Bobby Angelle (Ace Records)	Celeste
2008	An Introduction to Freddy Fender (Varese Sarabande)	Freddy Fender	Piano & Organ
2012	Boyo	Backyard Heavies	Piano & Organ
2012	Queen Sheba	Backyard Heavies	Organ

Made in the USA
Middletown, DE
27 October 2015